SPRITZING TO SUCCESS
with
the Woman Who Brought an Industry to Its
Senses

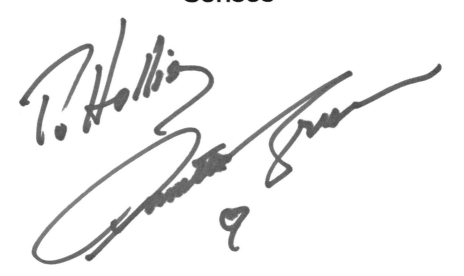

Annette Green

"High Priestess of the Fragrance World"*

First published by Dog Ear Publishing
4011 Vincennes Road
Indianapolis, IN 46268
www.dogearpublishing.net

ISBN: 978-1-4575-6540-3
Library of Congress Control Number: 2018951505

This book is printed on acid free paper.
Printed in the United States of America

To my mother, Mollie Green,
who taught me the power of love, personhood, perseverance,
patience, and perfume, although not necessarily in that order.

Exchanging hugs with
Rose Marie Bravo

As a young teenager growing up in the Bronx, (a borough of New York City), my best day was a Saturday when I would take the subway "downtown' to 59ᵗʰ Street and Lexington Avenue and enter Bloomingdale's and meander through the aisles and byways of its enormous perfume department.

Spritzing myself as I went along with all varieties of scents and potions, dabbing creams and lotions on any available part of the body. I was struck back then by the power of fragrance to evoke a memory or to conjure up visions of beauty and fantasy. The whiff of a scent with all its beautiful imagery and packaging, crystal bottles and elixir most powerfully could paint a picture, create a melody and, most amazingly, take me to another place. Little could I have dreamed that a decade later (1974-1987), I would be in charge of the country's largest purveyor of scents, 25 blocks south and a few blocks west at Herald Square as Macy's fragrance buyer. That is where I met and began my great friendship with the indefatigable and unstoppable Annette Green.

Annette Green and her life story in the realm of scents is a love story and a story of dreams coming true. How one woman took her passion for perfume and love of an industry, added courage, determination, drive and enormous talent and wit, and helped move it forward to today's global world of fragrance. An industry that was in its nascent stage of development, which consisted of disparate worlds of individual fragrance companies, many French and privately held, manufacturers, essential oil houses, perfumeries, department stores and marketing agencies. Annette helped to transform these powerful components and harmonize their efforts to work together for a bigger vision. She influenced how companies thought about products and marketing activities, visual display and education, focusing them to look both inward and outward. Annette dreamed big. She saw endless possibilities for this most powerful and elusive of the senses, the sense of smell.

She developed her own sixth sense to imagine what could be. Annette recognized the art of perfume making, scent, imagery and packaging creation and connected that creativity with science and olfactory experimentation and its outcomes: healing, ambience, mood creation and emotional well-being that fragrance can provide. She connected the dots with the commercial aspects of the business and engagement of consumers, taking them on the journey. Annette understood early that the experiences that are created at counters or on websites or in museums are what peak people's interest, and never more than now.

Spritzing to Success captures the names and faces of the times, the trends and changes in our society and early development of branding. In many ways, fragrance marketing and branding has been interpreted by other industries, along with the language and processes that were constructed over the last several decades in perfume launches.

Annette was at the forefront of developing a framework for the industry. She brought the worlds of theatre, art, film, science, and technology to the party. She helped the Foundation establish the guardrails of what constitutes success, through the FiFi's, the symposiums, the conferences, museum exhibitions and consumer educational events.

Annette is a force of nature. She has the determination, drive and persuasive powers and tenacity not to give up the dream. *Spritzing to Success* is inspiring as an American true grit story. As Leonard Lauder often says, "If you don't see the future, you will never get there."

Annette's book brought me right back to that Bloomingdale's counter, spritzing myself with the wonder and beauty of it all. Once more I fell in love with this amazing world of scents, and being in awe of the woman who made so many dreams come true.

Rose Marie Bravo
Former Chief Executive, Burberry (1997–2006)
Former President of Saks Fifth Avenue (1992–1997)

Sensory Strategies and Surprises

Backstory: Perfume in My Veins

Favorite Co-conspirators

Barney Zerbe, managing editor, *American Druggist*
George Bender, editorial director, *American Druggist*
Christine Chiossi, vice president of training, DuBarry/Richard Hudnut
Jack Mohr, vice president, Kings Men Toiletries, Richard Hudnut

> *Success is no accident. It is hard work, perseverance, learning, studying, sacrifice and most of all, love of what you are doing or learning to do.*
>
> **— Pelé**

Few treks to success have what it takes to lure the likes of superstars Elizabeth Taylor, Catherine Deneuve, and Sophia Loren into supporting roles.[1]

Greeting the glamorous Elizabeth Taylor.

Happily, mine did!

Thanks to the perfume passions of these legendary icons, our paths were destined to cross. The tipping point revealed itself one starry Paris night in the early seventies. I was sipping a light and fruity Beaujolais in a bistro on the Left Bank when, suddenly, a flight of fancy led me to an idea I had never had before. Could it be possible, I asked myself, for the Fragrance Foundation to give a sensory spin to the prerogative enjoyed by the movie and theatre worlds of honoring their own? There was no question in my mind that fragrance and its creation, packaging, and advertising were in the undisputed realm of artistry and deserved to be recognized. Little could I have imagined the awards (eventually dubbed the FiFis) would take on the aura of the Oscars and the Tonys and be embraced from here to Timbuktu.[2]

My forty-year journey through the world of the senses never stopped mixing the most amazing talents into my fragrance brew: authors (mystery story mavens Mary Higgins Clark and her daughter, Carol); a famous pop artist (Peter Max); sports stars (Frank Gifford and O. J. Simpson); supermodels (Carmen and Naomi Campbell); fashion designers (Karl Lagerfeld and Carolina Herrera); academics (Shirley Goodman, executive vice president/executive director, Educational Foundation for the Fashion Industries, and Dean Jack Rittenberg, the Fashion Institute of Technology); sensory specialists (Drs. Lewis Thomas, president emeritus, Memorial Sloan Kettering Cancer Center, and chairman of the board, Monell Chemical Senses Center, and Susan Schiffman, professor, medical psychology, Duke University Medical Center); futurists (Faith Popcorn and Edie Weiner, the Future Hunters); retail CEOs (Marvin Traub, Bloomingdale's, Rose Marie Bravo, Saks Fifth Avenue, and Helen Galland, Bonwit Teller). Even a famous astronaut (Buzz Aldrin) moved into my orbit, as well as a tycoon (Donald Trump) or two.

The fates played their part too. Not only did they deposit me in a time and place that was of little interest to anyone; they also gave me a head start, prenatally speaking.

The die was cast when my pregnant mother decided to hop on a bus from our home in Atlantic City in the early twenties to enjoy a shopping spree in Philadelphia. Her excursion was interrupted, however, when her amniotic sac, in which I was happily floating, suddenly burst right in the middle of the Perfume Department of Wanamaker's Department Store.

Everyone went into emergency mode. In the blink of an eye, we were safely ensconced in a nearby hospital. Several hours later, I made my debut.

After my mother recovered, we made our way back to Atlantic City, where we lived for another two or three years. My parents separated during that time, and mother moved us to my grandparent's home in Belleville, New Jersey: a small bedroom community at the edge of Newark. It was from that house at 162 Holmes Street that I could see the lights of the Empire State Building. I made up my mind then and there—Manhattan is where I belonged. I told everyone within earshot. In the interim, thanks to my mother (who was born in New York), I visited the city often and quickly became a "Broadway baby" and eager museum goer. My other childhood diversions included playing successful career woman. I made "important" calls every day to famous people around the world by disabling the telephone. I placed rubber bands on the buttons on the base of the phone so calls could still be made and received by anyone else in the house. When I wasn't making fantasy calls, I enjoyed publishing a neighborhood gossip sheet, picking and selling apples from my bicycle, running a lending library in the basement offering used comic and soft-cover books I had finished reading. I especially liked acting in plays at school and writing original sagas for home consumption starring my friends and me. Costumes were courtesy of my mother and ran the gamut from pirates to princesses.

As years flew by, I began to consider the possibility, plausible or not, that it was in the City of Brotherly Love my genes got scrambled and the most unappreciated of the senses—smell—came out on top. Admittedly, there was scant evidence from this serendipitous act of nature, that I would devote my grown-up life and career to the pleasures and rewards of the senses. Who can say what mysterious and invisible forces are at work in determining anyone's fortunes?[3]

Yet the question I have been asked more than any other remains: "How did an inexperienced 'stars in her eyes' twenty-something from Newark, New Jersey, turn into the muse of the international fragrance industry?"

Memories play tricks, but of one thing I am sure: My career climb took off just before WWII and was dedicated to the plebian task of learning the basics. I was energized by the "just get the job done well" lessons I absorbed in my first few years as a secretary. A short stint during the war as an executive assistant to a demanding but brilliant boss, J. Ernest Allen, in the New Jersey office of the Signal Corps set me on the straight and narrow. Considered a curmudgeon by his staff, I found J. Ernest witty, erudite, and worldly-wise. He was a tough but generous teacher, and after spending about a year in his domain, I was surprised and delighted to learn he had developed a very soft, even poetic, spot in his heart for me.[4]

The old cliché "Never judge a book by its cover" still stands me in good stead.

Once the war was over, everyone I knew was more than ready to get their lives back on track and in the process foster their passion for personal unfettered freedom. We were all searching for a space totally unlike any our parents had experienced. The "flower children" were waiting in the wings, and self-fulfillment was definitely in the air. Though I enjoyed the tumult of the changing society, I didn't let it sidetrack me.

Crossing the Hudson

Eager to hone my writing talents, I remained committed to the lure of New York City. It was a time when "work" had not yet become an ominous four-letter word and the possibility of finding a challenging career to love had "yes" written all over it. I made a spirited entry in the late fifties and landed a job as editorial assistant at the Hearst publication *American Druggist* on April Fool's Day. I must admit I did not consider that a good omen, but it was no joke—just not what I thought I wanted.

My mother (a 5'1" thumbs-up kind of person) suggested we make a practice run to Manhattan on the Sunday before I was scheduled to start my new job. She wanted to be sure I wouldn't get lost or arrive at work late. Allowing for a two-hour trip, we boarded a local bus from our New Jersey home, traveled to the Newark's Pennsylvania Station, caught the train to Manhattan, and in about a half hour, reached 34th Street. Our next challenge was to find the right subway to take us to the Hearst offices on 56th Street & Madison Avenue, but we did it. Satisfied (and relieved) with our success, we stopped for a sandwich and coffee at the counter in the then famous Halpern's Drug Store located in the Hearst Building, reversed our steps, and traveled back home. I was more than ready and eager to begin my new adventure.

I accepted the job at *American Druggist*, though my goal was to work for *Harper's Bazaar*. There were no openings. Personnel ("human resources" in today's vernacular) promised that when an editorial opportunity opened up at *Bazaar*, I would be at the top of the list. I agreed reluctantly.

My good fortune was to work for two caring and inspirational men at *American Druggist*: George Bender, who oversaw editorial content, and Barney Zerbe, the managing editor of the magazine. They pushed me to expand my horizons and gave me ever more difficult and demanding assignments. Some had nothing to do with druggists or the merchandise they sold. Barney urged me to research and write about the great actress Eva Le Gallienne and her repertory theater. I did, over and over again, until he was satisfied. It was really head-splitting, but I loved the challenge and the theater (a lifelong passion that fills my world today!). The Messrs. Bender and Zerbe never stopped encouraging me to do more, more. It was through their auspices that Hearst sent me to the private Shipman School of Journalism in the Times Building (the site of the famous New Year's Eve ball drop). I attended classes at the end of each day for two years, commuted home to New Jersey, and sold several articles under the guidance of my professor, Ida Leona Burleigh. One was based on an interview with Frank Lloyd Wright's younger sister, Maginel Wright Barney, who not only illustrated children's books but also designed and created incredibly beautiful jewel-encrusted velvet evening slippers.

I received a certificate of completion from the Shipman School at graduation ceremonies on the sprawling lawn of Anya Seton's Connecticut home. The best-selling author was basking in the success of her newest novel, *Dragonwyck*.

Without missing a step, I next signed up to attend night classes at New York University's School of Journalism. My mother made it possible by cashing in her World War II bonds. Without realizing it, I was preparing myself to fulfill dreams that I didn't even know I had. Nevertheless, my mind and heart were open to whatever might happen, and an awful lot certainly did.

Youthquake

My moment came in the late fifties when teenagers were beginning to emerge as habitués of the cosmetic and fragrance aisles of drugstores. It was where the top-of-the-line beauty and fragrance products were sold. In fact, perfumes (considered a precious luxury) were kept behind locked glass cases far from the reach of the consumer. Halpern's lunch counter was a favorite eatery for beautiful models and elegant society women. I often found myself joining them at the counter on my noon break. Perfect for glamorous people-watching. Just a block away, the Lilly Daché Millinery Salon added glamour to the neighborhood, which I especially appreciated because my mother had designed and sold hats at Bamberger's Department Store in Newark. As an aside, every woman who was a careerist, or wanted to be, always wore a hat, in and out of the office, all day long. It was considered *the* status symbol that separated the secretaries from those in executive positions. And how I loved those hats![5]

But hats were not on my mind while I worked for *American Druggist*. It was all about using my head to learn what it took to cover a story and produce readable, interesting, and insightful copy. Because I was the staff member on the magazine closest in age to the emerging teen consumer, one lucky day I was assigned a column dedicated to advising drugstore owners how to capitalize on the trend. The focus was the beauty-and-fragrance category. I convinced my local druggist in Newark to allow me to work behind the counter on weekends to get firsthand feedback. I also offered to dress the store's windows to catch the eye of this "hot" new shopper. Since I was a good customer, I was given carte blanche. The column was a success, and as the days and months went by, the inevitable happened. My fascination with fashion morphed into a fixation with the world of beauty. I was determined to learn as much as I could as fast as I could. And did I ever!

Beauty Biz

I gave my all at *American Druggist* for about a year and left with the blessings of my mentors. I realized it was the moment to educate myself on what the beauty industry was all about. I was lucky enough to be offered a job at Richard Hudnut/DuBarry, at the time a powerful American-based beauty-and-fragrance company. Its Manhattan offices were housed in a gigantic restructured warehouse on Seventh Avenue and Eighteenth Street. Before I knew it, I was on the fast track to becoming a beauty industry insider. My first assignment was to write a fashion/beauty-inspired newsletter, which the company distributed to the ladies who attended the DuBarry Success School on Fifth Avenue. An elegant salon specializing in diet, exercise, and overall fitness, as well as skin and hair care, it was ruled by Ann Delafield, an eccentric but extraordinary woman in the style of Helena Rubinstein and Elizabeth Arden. Miss Delafield commanded an army of experts and demanded fealty and dedication to her ideal of American beauty. Women came from far and wide to practice what she preached. She reigned unchallenged by corporate management—threatening to jump out the window if anyone disagreed with her. On more than one occasion, I saw her run over to the nearest window to carry out her threat. Fortunately, the DuBarry executives always capitulated before she could take action.

Her clothes, which she had custom made, were a miracle of modern American technology. A mold was made of her body and given to her dressmaker, who created a wardrobe Miss Delafield could just step into—no need for bras and other underpinnings. I was fascinated by this woman and her demands. The overwhelming success of her avant-garde ideas about beauty led the company to develop what became a mail-order version based on the regimes taught in the Fifth Avenue Salon. Women across the country eagerly subscribed to get their at-home beauty and fitness fix. They were encouraged to follow up with visits to local retailers to purchase the prescribed DuBarry essentials. That's where I came in. It was my job to expand Success School coverage in the newsletter I wrote, specifically for mail-order subscribers, as well as provide a platform for their questions and suggestions. When I think about it from the vantage point of today's world, the long-forgotten Ann Delafield probably created the template for many in the industry to follow. How astounded she would be with the twenty-first century emphasis on her concepts of inner and outer beauty.

After about six months, I was recruited to write materials for the company's behind-the-counter sales specialists. I could not have been happier. It meant I would be working for the brilliant (and elegant) head of the department, Christine Chiossi. She became my mentor and lifelong role model. To me, she was the epitome of a successful woman executive: self-confident, totally knowledgeable, and vigorous. She had a down-to-earth, no-nonsense style that was extremely kind and inspirational. How lucky I was to have her take me under her wing. She was more than willing to teach me everything I wanted to know, which was *everything*! Her generosity of spirit made learning easy and fun. Time became irrelevant. I was ready to work around the clock if need be. As her sales training writer,

I was assigned the task of interpreting her philosophy and incorporating it into advice about products and selling techniques for the company's retail sales representatives. My responsibilities also included writing selling materials for the Kings Men toiletries division, headed by another top executive, Jack Mohr. A charming, erudite man who always reminded me of the much-admired crooner of the forties and fifties, Bing Crosby, I found working with him a joy and an inspiration. As luck would have it, he would become a guiding force in my life, eventually making all things possible.

During my sojourn at the company, I became infatuated with fragrance. What really captured my heart was an exquisitely written book, *The Romance of Perfume* by Richard Le Gallienne, exotically illustrated by George Barbier. Published in France by Richard Hudnut in 1928, it included many fascinating and poetic passages, which I still refer to. M. Le Gallienne reveled in the thought that "some philosophers, indeed, have placed the soul in the olfactory nerve, and the sense of smell has always been recognized as the most ethereal of the senses." I was in total agreement.

I settled in for the long haul. My plans were about to change, however, when out-of-the-blue job offers began to fill my in-box. I hesitated to leave. I was so happy and fulfilled in my job, I felt it would make me look ungrateful. After a heartfelt talk about my future, Miss Chiossi urged me to spread my wings. I did—with a vengeance.

It wasn't until the mid-fifties, after I had worked in New York for a couple of years, earning a small but decent living, that I jumped ship to become a full-fledge Manhattanite (to no one's surprise except, surprisingly, my mother's?) and rented a postage-stamp-size apartment on 30th Street between Lexington and Third Avenues. The magical aura of Manhattan filled me with awe each and every day. I was in love, and I didn't keep it a secret. There wasn't an imperfection in sight. What a time to be young, focused, and open to the thrills of the city and its mesmerizing beat. All my dreams of becoming a "real" New Yorker were coming true.

I spent a lot of time in Greenwich Village in those early days, absorbing what to me was artistic heaven. Inspirational voices filled every nook and cranny above and below the cobblestone streets. Coffee shops welcomed poets and musicians who performed for free without being asked. The Village drew young people from around the country. Making friends who had the same passion for the city and what it had to offer couldn't have been easier. We enjoyed discovering the ways of the world and our chances in it. Falling in love (often with each other) was the order of the day. Not surprisingly, the intensity of all that emotion was doomed to sputter, and it did. After about a year or so, the group scattered and disappeared into the canyons of Manhattan, never to be seen again.

At this point, I had joined the Editorial Department of MacFadden Publication on 42nd Street. The commute to my office, on the Third Avenue El, allowed me a clandestine look into people's windows and their lives. At MacFadden I was not only the beauty and fashion editor but book and movie reviewer, as well. Contributing to their racy stable of magazines (*True Love*, *True Experiences*, *True Story*, *True Romance*, and the celebrity-skewed *Photoplay*) was like being caught in a firestorm.

To recover from burnout, after about a year in the trenches, I decided to try my hand at freelancing. I wasn't making much of a living, and I definitely didn't like working alone in my small apartment. An unexpected telephone call was manna from heaven. A woman who identified herself as Gail Dugas, the women's page editor of NEA (the syndicated arm of Scripps Howard News Service), explained she was looking for an assistant, and a colleague had recommended me. I had no idea who this mysterious benefactor was, but I leaped at the opportunity. Not only was I responsible for weekly coverage of the beauty and fragrance worlds but I was assigned interviews with famous celebs of the day. One of the most memorable was meeting the irresistible Frank Sinatra at a recording studio. (Years before, I had been one of the "bobby-soxers" standing for hours to hear him sing at the Paramount.) I was thrilled to watch as he joined the opera star Risë Stevens in a medley of pop songs and later interview him about the session. What I especially remember was the long-stemmed rose he gave me. He certainly lived up to his "heartthrob" billing. I floated down Park Avenue, showing the rose to every doorman I passed and, of course, telling each the story.

Another ladies' man I interviewed was the glamorous Ezio Pinza, who was starring in the 1940's hit show *South Pacific*. Once again I found myself in a recording studio. This time, Mr. Pinza was nowhere in sight. I must have waited an hour. He finally arrived with a rather large entourage. As we moved as a group toward a conference room, I suddenly looked up at Mr. Pinza, who towered over me, and blurted out, "I cannot interview with an audience." He laughed and advised his ten or so associates to wait outside. The interview lasted for almost an hour and he couldn't have been more forthcoming, interested, and interesting. We discussed everything from his life on stage to our mutual love of *The Little Prince* by Saint Exupery.

Just twelve months into this most enjoyable assignment, Jack Mohr reappeared to pluck me out of the high-spirited world of newsmakers that I was savoring with such fervor.

As it turned out, after we had both left DuBarry, Jack had become president of Lentheric Perfumes. A division of Squibb, it was the US distributor of beautiful fragrances, including Tweed, which was enjoying considerable popularity at the time. One day Jack saw my byline in the Scripps Howard paper, the *New York World Telegram and Sun*, and called to see if I was the same Annette Green he had known at Hudnut. As soon as he found out I was, he invited me to lunch. By the time we reached dessert, Jack invited me to be his public relations director. I assured him I was unqualified, but he was persistent and confident I would find out how to do the job. Of course, I did. Fortunately, I had a bunch of magazine beauty editor buddies, newspaper business editors, and PR mavens were more than eager to give me a crash course.

I thoroughly enjoyed the fast-paced days and nights demanded in the public relations world. I never could have imagined how grateful I would be to Jack. Under his tutelage I learned the power of celebrities and how to reach and convince them to participate in events we were planning to promote our fragrances. Jack loved glamorous parties, and more often than not they were held in the exclusive Hermès boutique on the ground floor of our elegant six-story building on the corner of Fifth Avenue and 53rd Street. The lush setting, behind floor-to-ceiling glass walls, was a magnet for the most celebrated personalities. Among his favorites was the voluptuous American mezzo-soprano Jean Madeira. Admired by the opera world (including the Met) for her magnificent portrayal of Carmen, she regularly attended our press events and glamorous nights on the town. Sadly, her future was unfulfilled because of her unexpected death in her early fifties.

Jack asked me at one point to invite Marlene Dietrich to join one of the events. The German-born chanteuse, movie star, and sex symbol was glamour personified. Beginning in the thirties, she had made an indelible mark in the entertainment world, and that mark lasted throughout her long life. I had

Here I am receiving a shipment of Lentheric perfumes from Paris.

A night of celebration with, left to right, Jack Mohr, President of Lentheric, opera star Jean Madeira, Bill Canaday, Executive Vice-President of Lentheric and me.

met Miss Dietrich several times during her shopping trips to the Hermès boutique. Whenever celebrities appeared, it was my job to welcome them and be as helpful as possible. We met again at the opening of the play *House of Flowers* starring the brilliant performer Pearl Bailey. I was invited backstage as a perk for having arranged to have Lentheric provide floral fragrances for the audience on opening night. During the performance, Miss Bailey suddenly forgot the lyrics to one of the songs. It was a hair-raising moment. After the show, I found her sobbing in the arms of Marlene Dietrich, who was gently comforting her. I still remember Miss Dietrich looking ravishing in a figure-hugging pale-green silk gown with a tremendous self-fabric bow at her waist. It was quite a scene. Despite being charming to us all, however, Miss Dietrich never did agree to attend a Lentheric event.

The forties movie heartthrob Tyrone Power did. I invited him to be photographed for an Easter promotional shoot with his then movie actress wife, Linda Christian, and their baby daughter, Romina. The setting was staged in front of a lilac-filled fountain in the lobby of the Savoy Plaza Hotel on Fifth Avenue. A hit with the press, the tie-in was a real coup for Lentheric's newest fragrance, Red Lilac.

Jack sent me on my first trip to Paris to see for myself how Parisians shopped and enjoyed fragrance. I stayed in the Hotel Bristol, which at the time was a tiny version of its current grandeur. Still, the art nouveau grated elevator remains a poignant reminder of the way it was. I relished the sights, sounds, and smells of Paris. I was besotted. Paris is the only city I ever visited that left me in tears as the plane rolled down the runway to take me home. It took many months for me to find emotional footing again as I readjusted to my bustling life in Manhattan.

Happily, a year later I had the opportunity to return. My assignment this time was to chaperone the winner of a beauty contest the company had sponsored to find a glamour girl to represent its new "Miss Pippin" lipstick. The winner, who looked remarkably like a young Marilyn Monroe, hailed from Athens, Georgia. The trip took us to Paris and

Ireland. It was challenging but great fun. I wasn't prepared, however, for the effect this voluptuous blonde bombshell would have wherever we went. She stopped traffic on the Champs-Élysées as a multitude of men of all ages and persuasions surrounded us. Though she reveled in the attention, I found myself on a round-the-clock nerve-racking watch.

Finally, I was given a car to drive us wherever. It helped but driving in Paris was hardly fun. After a four-day visit, we left the city for Dublin, where we were in the capable hands of the Browns, a husband-and-wife team affiliated with Lentheric. They gave us the royal treatment on a drive through the breathtakingly beautiful green countryside. It included, of course, kissing the Blarney Stone. Our final destination was Shannon, where we boarded our plane home. The next challenge was to arrange for my charge's trip back to Athens. She wasn't eager to leave. My mother joined us in Pennsylvania Station to give me moral support. I needed it as men lined up on facing benches in the waiting room. Relief came with the aid of my straight-laced mother, who took charge of the situation and had us wait for the train in the ladies' room. As I watched the train pull away, it was clear that I learned more than I could have ever anticipated about the responsibility of being responsible.

Once my life got back to normal, working at Lentheric set me on a path to an extraordinary career that lay ahead. I never looked for another job. I was just swept along as the company changed hands over the next few years. Squibb sold Lentheric to Olin-Matheson, and I found myself working with a brilliant group of ex-newspaper pros in the high-powered Public Relations Department of the corporation. It was there that I really learned what dealing with the press was all about. Responsibilities included promoting everything from Winchester guns to roller skates to perfumes. My in-house reputation soared when I convinced the Henri Bendel specialty store (then located on Fifty-Seventh Street) to mount an African promotion, complete with windows featuring mannequins dressed for a safari and equipped with Winchesters. Top brass was delighted. I settled in for the long haul.

Once again, it wasn't to be. Another move was in the wings when Chicago-based Helene Curtis acquired Lentheric, and I went along as part of the package to handle PR and promotional activities in their New York office. In no time at all, I was developing publicity campaigns for do-it-yourself home permanents, hair-care products, deodorants, men's toiletries, and, of course, the perfumes of Lentheric. It was a wonderfully stimulating time. I was disappointed, to say the least, when the company announced it was planning to shutter the New York office and move everyone to the Windy City. I opted out. Corporate life (and leaving New York) was not for me.

On My Own

Colleagues encouraged me to establish my own marketing and public relations agency, which I decided was worth a try after getting the go-ahead from my accountant, on whom I always depended for financial advice. Helene Curtis made it easy and inexpensive too. They sold me desks, typewriters, and file cabinets for a pittance. They arranged for their advertising agency, Altman Stoller, to become my first client. In a matter of months, I was more than ready to move into a small two-room space (with its own entrance), which was part of an advertising agency's offices in the old Architects Building at 101 Park Avenue. The building, a stolid male bastion, had so few ladies' rooms that we had to travel four or five floors by elevator to reach one.

I opened Annette Green Associates for business in the early sixties with just a secretary. The agency grew so fast that I moved four times to ever-larger spaces. Even the building's staff applauded. After about a year, I was joined by a close friend and colleague, Lois Berk, whom I had met and worked with at Helene Curtis. She invested in the agency and became a partner. Her savvy business acumen and behind-the-scenes talents allowed me the freedom to devote my energies to developing services and creative programs for our increasing roster of clients. A constant flurry of recommendations from the beauty, fashion, and business press was the key to our overnight success.

My fledging agency's first remarkable stroke of luck was triggered by a phone call from a Dr. Thomas Bishop. He was the head of the French Department at New York University and its French House (La Maison Francaise) at 16 Washington Mews between Fifth Avenue and University Place. The historic cobblestone street, lined with 1800s carriage houses, has long been a favorite Washington Square attraction. The call, Dr. Bishop explained, was prompted by a suggestion of a colleague who knew about me and my new agency. His query was whether or not I could produce a French carnival on the Mews to raise funds to support the French-American cultural activities of the Maison. Without hesitation, I said yes.

After several meetings with the charming and erudite Dr. Bishop, my agency was chosen, and I embarked on what turned out to be a most fanciful and creative assignment. To lend a Gallic air to the evening, I researched and found a leading Broadway lighting designer who agreed to create French flags in red, white, and blue lights to line the length of both sides of the Mews. Once we received permission from Con Edison to draw power from a source on Fifth Avenue, we were on our way. I had a stage built in the middle of the Mews for a small dance band and the artists who would perform. Our star on that magical night was the fabulous American jazz singer, Bricktop. Like Josephine Baker, she had moved to France because of racial barriers to find her fame and fortune. Her singing and dancing caused a sensation, and when she opened a namesake nightclub, it became the talk of Paris. Fortunately for me, she had just returned to the States to stay. What a memorable performance she gave as she sang a string of favorites, including many by Cole Porter. (As an aside, he had written "Miss Otis Regrets" especially for her.)

To add to the carnival atmosphere, we rented bare-bones convention-style booths and decorated them with red, white, and blue crepe paper. Everyone we could corral helped, including mothers, sisters, husbands, and friends. When the gala night came, the weather was perfect, and the night sky was star-struck. The booths, placed along the perimeter of the Mews opposite the carriage houses, were ready for action. Sponsored by several luxury goods companies, they offered attendees an assortment of pleasures, including food, drinks, and delightful games of chance. One of the booths was run by the famous Librairie de France bookstore, which at the time was a landmark destination at Rockefeller Center. There were elegant prizes to be won, provided by the companies and several of my clients. Guests also enjoyed the opportunity to visit many of the private houses on the Mews. The carnival was such an overwhelming success that my agency was retained to do repeat performances for two more years.

The second year was a smash, too, with the acclaimed cabaret songstress, Wisconsin-born Hildegarde, singing favorites, including her most famous, "Darling, Je Vous Aime Beaucoup." A glamorous icon, she always added to the romantic ambiance by playing the piano wearing her signature long white gloves (shades of Liberace who, by the way, reportedly was inspired by her high style). An extra added attraction the second year was made possible by the residents of the Mews, who opened their "secret" gardens located behind the carriage houses so guests could dine under a canopy of multicolored lights, which we strung through the branches of the trees. What a glorious night that was. Unfortunately, the third year we were unmercifully rained out. No more carnivals after that. Even so, it was an incredible experience for us all. Profitable too!

Inspired by what we had accomplished and the terrific media coverage, the agency moved on and up.

Another assignment that brought us attention was an "only in New York" happening we produced for Breck Shampoo and their famous ad campaign featuring memorable artists' renderings of the so-called Breck Girls. My task was to keep Breck in the news—not easy for a beauty product. Yet, in one instance, we did just that by making a small but positive dent in an event which otherwise was shameful. The year was 1970, and the anxieties of the Vietnam War and the racial tragedy that had erupted at Kent University had reached a boiling point. During the early morning hours of May 8 (which the press dubbed "Bloody Friday"), two hundred construction workers, reportedly organized by the New York State AFL/ CIO, gathered in lower Manhattan for the express purpose of breaking up a peaceful protest being held by over one thousand high school and college students. The resulting media coverage headlined the debacle "The Hard Hat Riot." Over twenty policemen and students were hurt. It caused an uproar from coast to coast. If ever the image of hard hats needed repatriation, it was at that moment in time. At a meeting with the Breck team, I proposed we reach out to the construction foreman of a midtown site to invite a group of his workers to show their softer side by participating in a girl-watching lunchtime survey. The idea was to have them help select a dozen or so passersby with particularly beautiful hair as Breck Girls. They welcomed the opportunity, and by the time lunch hour was over, winners were chosen to the applause of a swelling audience of sidewalk kibitzers. Each winner was gifted with a year's supply of Breck products, and the hard hats who participated received the same to bring home to their families. Press coverage and public reaction proved positive for everyone involved.

The first fragrance client awarded the agency was Corday Perfumes, thanks to its president, Herbert Storfer. Though it was a relatively small account, I relished the possibility of promoting its famous perfume, Toujours Moi. What a monumental opportunity this account would turn out to be. In the blink of an eye, Corday was acquired by Max Factor. I was worried when I learned the public relations for the West Coast-based company was in the hands of the renowned international fashion authority, Eleanor Lambert. For unknown reasons, however, the California cosmetics giant decided to realign with a small agency, and happily, Annette Green Associates was it.

What a marvelous long-running relationship we had. During the more than ten years we represented the company, our efforts were rewarded with major press coverage for all the company's many products and promotional efforts, including the admired Max Factor Museum in Hollywood. I worked under the direction of Bill Hardwick, a charming and wise six-footer who was the public relations manager of the company. I had the pleasure, too, of interacting with Chet Firestein and his brother, Alfred, who helmed Max Factor (both the founder's nephews). Over the years, I came to treasure their expressions of appreciation for our work on the company's behalf. I still have one of the handwritten notes Bill sent me at holiday time in 1972:

> Dear Annette: It doesn't seem possible that so many years have passed since I first met the tiny little miss with the tall, green-trimmed hat in the Pierre dining room—for lunch with Alfred. I always look back to that day and never have regretted our decision to go with Annette

Green and Associates. *We* have had another wonderful association throughout 1972 and both Alfred and Chet, of course, I feel the same way. We send you best wishes for the happiest of holidays and the greatest year of all in '73—and so do all your other friends at Max Factor. Thanks again for everything.

As you can imagine, Corday always got my special attention. For a few years, one of our most lauded efforts took place on Bastille Day (July 14) in New York's Central Park. It revolved around a puppet show I wrote starring Toujours Moi as the heroine in a Parisian love story. I luckily discovered a wonderfully talented puppeteer to produce the show. It became a star attraction on the Naumberg Bandstand Stage, located near the Bethesda Fountain between 66th and 72nd Streets. The charming puppets and the story of their romance turned out to be a favorite with families and tourists who happened to be in the Park. My mother, who helped with all our events, was always seated upfront in the audience and was enchanted by the performance—even though she had seen it many times at rehearsals. We distributed Toujours Moi perfume samples to members of the audience, and all in all, the show turned out to be a low-key promotional success.

In the early sixties, we were also retained to represent a Boston-based group affiliated, as I remember, with the Joseph P. Kennedy Foundation. The extraordinary Eunice Shriver Kennedy (President Kennedy's sister, internationally renowned for founding the Special Olympics) was the executive vice president of the foundation. Our responsibility was to promote the work of young artists who had been taken under the wing of a committee known today as the President's Committee for People with Intellectual Disabilities. Despite the challenges, their work was quite wonderful. I was proud to hang several of their creative and beautifully executed paintings and drawings in my office.

As a jumping-off point, I proposed an exhibition of their work at the prestigious Weintraub Art Gallery on Madison Avenue. I had met Jacob Weintraub years earlier when I first came to the city and often hung out in his small gallery and frame shop, which was close to one of my first apartments on Lexington Avenue. He and his wife became friends. I was sure he would help, and he did. To give the project even more weight, I spoke to Larry Gordon, the president of another client, Blue Ridge Winkler Textiles, about the possibility of creating prints based on the artists' renderings, which would eventually be featured in the company's fabric collections. Sales would benefit the artists. He agreed, too. Once the fabrics were produced, we framed each design to hang in the Weintraub Gallery next to the artwork it had inspired.

What really turned the event into a big-time newsmaker was my request to the foundation to have Rose Kennedy, the president's mother, attend the opening. The answer was yes! As you can guess, we knew we had a blockbuster on our hands. I alerted the TV news desks and the print media. At first, they were rather dubious, to say the least. But I had them check the foundation for proof positive.

We were set to meet Mrs. Kennedy at about 10:00 a.m. at the gallery on a Saturday morning. It was full of TV cameras and reporters when I arrived about 8:00. The hours began to fly by, but no Rose Kennedy. The camera crews were getting restless and more than a bit hostile. I had that sinking feeling she may have changed her mind. At about one o'clock, a beaten-up yellow taxi arrived (I was looking for a limo) and out stepped daughter Eunice Shriver Kennedy, who turned to help her mother. As soon as they were inside, we were asked to pay the fare, since they had no money between them. I couldn't have been happier to comply. Mrs. Kennedy then asked me to hold her extremely heavy alligator handbag. Free of the burden, she blithely took the reporters and the camera crews up a flight of stairs to the second floor (no elevator for her) where all the drawings and paintings were hung. She stopped in front of each one to carefully describe the artist and explain his or her challenges. Everyone was totally inspired. I have to say, to be in the presence of Mrs. Kennedy was otherworldly. She had a transfixing aura that we all immediately sensed. It was an experience I am certain everyone involved still treasures. I know I do.

The Art of the Heart

Despite the intensity of building a business from scratch, I always spared time for the philanthropic side of my life. One of the most rewarding was an affiliation in the early sixties with the Blue Curtain Youth Foundation. It worked out of the Middle Collegiate Church at 50 East 7th Street in lower Manhattan. Founded as a nonprofit in 1955, the foundation was the brainchild of Katherine Anderson, a tender-hearted, socially conscious cheerleader for "disadvantaged children and young people of every race, creed and religion." Right up my alley. Blue Curtain operated—free of charge—during after-school hours, evenings, and Saturdays from October to June. Practicing professionals did the teaching—pro bono, of course. That's where I came in.

Miss Anderson invited me to teach a course in grooming, fashion, and modeling. At the time, about two hundred of the poorest of the poor children from every borough of the city were enrolled. They came from the streets, family courts, city shelters, and welfare institutions. Classes in ballet, modern dance, and acrobatics were taught by professionals in each discipline, through a grant from the Rebekah Harkness Foundation. There were pros teaching art and the techniques of playing baseball and boxing. I also served on the board's steering committee. I couldn't have been more enthusiastic. Not only was I eager to participate but it allowed me to take advantage of my fashion and beauty connections. My class of about twenty-five preteen girls was difficult to communicate with. The girls were dispirited, shy, and resentful; basically, a feeling of hopelessness pervaded the auditorium. I not only had to break through the sad state of affairs but find a way to give each girl the confidence to stand on the stage, face an audience of friends, family, and teachers at the conclusion of the course, and clearly announce her name, age, and ambition. At first this seemed like an impossible task. I couldn't even encourage most of the girls to speak to me. Several hid under their coats and jackets, which they put over their heads to block out any possible interaction between us. I found myself ducking under those barriers to try to begin even the simplest conversation, starting with "hello." Nevertheless, as time went by, with gentle persuasion, the class came to believe I really wanted to help them. Although it was unbelievably hard, each girl was eventually able to stand on the stage and announce who she was and what she hoped to be. One of the carrots I used was the promise of receiving brand-new clothes to wear and, most importantly, keep. I invited colleagues from the beauty and fashion worlds to be guest lecturers and to donate clothes and grooming products. By June, the girls were totally in my corner and eager to participate. I can only say the presentation went off without a hitch, and we ended the day with lots of hugs and kisses. When I think about it now and realize the need for caring hearts is still a major issue, I can't help wondering if the legacy of Katherine Anderson couldn't and shouldn't be revived to bring hope and encouragement to today's needy young girls. It is a promise I am making to myself to try.

My volunteer efforts also included visiting hospitals and therapy centers. What I learned (and never forgot) was the need, once a person was feeling better, for cosmetics, fragrance, a hair brush, and comb. I didn't want to leave the men out, either, because I realized they were on the road to recovery, too, when they asked for shaving essentials, cologne, and items to spruce up their hair. This was definitely a business I knew I would thrive in.

It was to my fast-growing agency that the fragrance industry's keepers of the flame turned to help save the Fragrance Foundation.

As with all adventurous undertakings, the moon and stars have to be aligned in your favor, especially when you are committed to climbing the highest mountain. Luckily, I found myself in the right place at the right time. As an extra bonus, the gods blessed me with a remarkably good sense of timing. I needed all the help I could get—from wherever, whoever. What moved the needle was a bundle of outside forces that fell in my lap: a dynamic societal upheaval, an American public and fragrance world yet to appreciate their full power and the potential of all those collective noses, as well as a subliminal desire by those at the top to be recognized for the industry's artistry and marketing breakthroughs. Behind the scenes, I heard growing chatter from a bevy of corporate suitors (with deep pockets) who wanted to share the rewards of what was perceived to be the sweet smell of success. The potential was limitless. By the end of the seventies, all bets were off. To add to the excitement, the trip was packed with the most creative, dynamic, and star-studded fellow travelers. I revved up my inner engine and never stopped to catch my breath.

The wisdom of the great Roman poet, Virgil, is advice worth pondering:

"Believe one who has proved it: believe in an expert."

1. The Game Changer, chapter 4.
2. *The Game Changer*, chapter 4.
3. "It is only with the heart that one sees rightly.
   What is essential is invisible to the eye."
   Antoine de Saint-Exupery, *The Little Prince*.
4. Mr. Allen wrote a poem just as I was getting ready to leave for my first job in Manhattan:
   "Oh! Annette Green
   Oh! Annette Green
   Were it not that I have a good wife,
   I would take you away in a flying machine,
   And we would fly for the rest of my life."
5. To be in the game, I had to acquire a wardrobe of chapeaux. Luckily, I discovered a shop on West 55th Street in Manhattan that turned out to be a haven for heavenly headgear. The domain of a talented retailing guru, Miriam Rigler, her shop boasted an inventory of every imaginary design. Her specialty was soft fedoras, straw bowlers, charming cloches, and an endless array of flower-bedecked confections in velvet, cotton, rayon, and silk. I was like the proverbial kid in a candy store. I guess I caught the millinery gene from my mother, because I became a real devotee. It didn't take long for me to search for a style that would be mine alone. At the time I was fascinated by the image of ancient Egypt's Queen Nefertiti (still am!) and her famous headdress. Only Miriam could have helped me fulfill my fantasy. Before I knew it, I was the custodian of custom-designed creations in the shape of the famous queen's "stovepipe" headdress. I have to admit that they were not easy to wear and had to be anchored to my hair with long bobby pins. Nevertheless, I loved each and every one, although I did buy a gold-tone hat stand for my desk so I could doff the "madcap" of the day from time to time. When the fashion for hats faded in the late sixties, I stowed my collection and joined the new trend to big hair-dos, which were mercilessly teased and coaxed to amazing heights. Miriam refocused her business and became the source for beautifully edited clothes for work, play, and grand evenings. She dressed me for every occasion during all those years at the Fragrance Foundation and not only fulfilled my "FiFi" costume dreams but helped me build a wardrobe that took me around the world with total confidence. I still find myself wearing most of what I bought from Miriam. Timeless!

I

Daring Rescue

Favorite Co-conspirators

Joseph Danilek, president of Mary Chess Fragrances
Paul Martineau, president of Caron
Jack Mohr, vice president, Fragrance Division, Revlon
Ernest Shifton, master perfumer, International Flavors & Fragrances
Thomas B. Haire, publisher of the trade magazine *Cosmetics and Toiletries*
William Randall, president, Sea & Ski
Rebecca McGreevey, vice president of public relations, Estée Lauder
Edie Weiner, president of the Future Hunters (formerly Weiner, Edrich, Brown)
Margaret Mead, curator emeritus of ethnology of the American Museum of Natural History

There are some things one can only achieve by a leap in the opposite direction.

— Franz Kafka

When I was asked to save the defunct Fragrance Foundation, it certainly was not for money. There was none!

The drama began just as I was sitting down to lunch with an editorial colleague at the Doral Hotel on Park Avenue in Manhattan. Before we could order, the waiter advised me I had an urgent call from my office. Since smartphones were yet to be invented, I picked up the landline at the reception desk. My partner, Lois Berk, quickly briefed me on a conversation she had just had with my long-time mentor and friend, Jack Mohr. He wanted to know if it was possible for me to drop whatever I was doing and hurry up to Peacock Alley at the Waldorf Astoria. It seemed a committee dedicated to saving the Fragrance Foundation was waiting to meet me. It came as quite a surprise, since I had no idea the foundation needed saving.

Fortunately, my luncheon companion was very understanding and encouraged me to do whatever. I rushed out of the hotel, crossed Park Avenue, hailed a cab, and in moments was at the Waldorf.

Ensconced in the Peacock Alley bar were four industry leaders: Joseph Danilek (Mary Chess), Paul Martinot (Caron), Sydney Friend (International Flavors & Fragrances), and, of course, Jack. He introduced me to the group. Mr. Danilek explained that the purpose of the meeting was to decide whether or not to close down the moribund Fragrance Foundation. The question hanging in the air, I quickly learned, was whether or not I would be willing to take the floundering organization under my wing— pro bono. Oddly enough, I felt it was not outside the realm of reason. I couldn't think of a valid reason why my fast-growing marketing-and-public-relations agency, Annette Green Associates, couldn't (shouldn't) take in the desperate orphan. Jack Mohr's role in the negotiations swayed my decision. He had made it perfectly clear I was "the person to rescue the foundation." It was definitely in character that Jack would think of me. He had been a supporter from the moment I met him in the fifties when we were both working at Richard Hudnut/DuBarry.

No one at the meeting hid the sad state of affairs of the foundation. The organization was basically penniless and out of business. It had no members, no board, no nothing except invaluable historical files. They had been housed with Helen Nash Associates, a public relations agency hired as a last resort when the foundation's offices were shuttered in the late fifties. What a comedown after what was certainly an auspicious beginning in 1949. The Fragrance Foundation was created as a nonprofit, educational organization by six great perfume and cosmetic houses (Chanel, Coty, Elizabeth Arden, Guerlain, Helena Rubinstein, and Parfums Weil). Their challenge was to build what was then a small, low-six-figure business in the American market. In fact, just three new fragrances were introduced that year: Diorama by Christian Dior, English Leather by MEM, and Moustache by Parfums Rochas.

Hard Sell

My first encounter with the Fragrance Foundation happened in the mid-fifties. I was invited to attend the fifth annual convention of the organization as a reporter for *American Druggist* magazine. The chairman of the convention was Thomas B. Haire. He reviewed the growth and achievements of the foundation since its creation five years earlier. He posed the provocative question, "Are members of the foundation getting their money's worth from their membership? Yes, you are getting your money's worth and then some! There is not a single city in the United States of twenty thousand or more population where newspapers haven't carried some word to their readers about fragrances. The foundation covers all markets, not only with newspaper editorials but also with radio, TV, and magazine coverage." He pointed out that though the foundation was originally conceived as a public relations organization, "it now also functions as a sales training agency, bureau of information, and a sales promotion organization."

The attendees of the convention were also shown *Fragrance for Living and Giving*, a consumer film that was being made available to schools and women's clubs, as well as TV stations and stores. The message focused on educating American women about the pleasures of perfume, its romantic history, and how to wear and take care of what was then considered a precious luxury. The meeting and the message were impressive.

Yet the founding members still had a lot of convincing to do. The industry was not clear as to the necessity of supporting the newly-established foundation. In its first year, a luncheon meeting attracted members of the powerful cosmetics trade group, the Toilet Goods Association.[1] The purpose was to brief leaders on how the organization would link consumers, retailers, media, and manufacturers in a comprehensive, nationwide educational campaign promoting perfumes and the secrets of how French women wore and took care of them. It was designed to win over the industry emotionally and financially.

At the time, a dedicated woman, Miriam Gibson French, was the coordinator for all Fragrance Foundation activities. Her responsibility was to expand appreciation of fragrance, especially French perfumes, which dominated the small market. She worked with the press, traveled throughout the country, and made presentations to women's club members, school students, cosmetic buyers, and salesgirls in retail stores. Since most fragrances were sold in high-end, privately owned drugstores and displayed behind locked glass doors, Mrs. French was determined to get those doors unlocked so the perfumes would be more accessible to shoppers. It didn't happen for many years.

TV Takedown

Despite considerable progress in establishing the foundation as a force for building the use of fragrance in the American market, by the end of the decade, the Fragrance Foundation fell on hard times. Whatever the reasons, the final blow was struck at another press conference I attended in the mid-fifties. It previewed the launch of one of the first TV commercials to be produced in or out of the fragrance industry. With much fanfare, the French-led group unveiled what turned out to be a rather ill-conceived commercial. The theme was "Tick-tock, wear fragrance 'round the clock," and the visual, as I recall, was dominated by an oversize, unattractive wall clock ticking away. I didn't know much about TV or commercials in those days, but in my heart of hearts, I felt that this one was not going to be successful. Unfortunately, I was right. So much money had been spent on the failed commercial, it spawned a quarrel over whose fault it had been. In the blink of an eye, the founders resigned and left the foundation afloat in a leaderless sea of red ink. Finding themselves with no money, the self-appointed committee of saviors were faced with a do-or-die conundrum.

It was Jack Mohr who sealed the foundation's fate—as well as my own. Certainly, there could have been another rescuer, but as fortune would have it, I was the one. In 1962, the committee appointed me executive director with the proviso that I would be able to maintain my agency as a separate entity. At a follow-up meeting, however, I realized they hadn't come to grips with how we were going to interact. They were bandying around the possibilities. Ignoring my presence, one of the committee members assured the others I was "a nice little lady," implying I would do what I was told.

I could feel a red-hot flush as I pulled myself up to my full five feet, three inches and in the strongest voice I could muster, blurted out, "Gentleman, I am *not* a 'nice little lady.' I am a tough, experienced, and successful businesswoman. I will do everything possible to save the foundation, but you must give me free rein." They were taken aback, but since they had no idea what to do, they retreated and left the fate of the foundation in my hands.

Rescue Operations

My charge was to resuscitate the Fragrance Foundation, which had been a perfect-pitched public voice in the service of the elegant (but small) perfume industry in the United States. It was founded in 1949 to change the fortunes of the high-priced, low-volume French-dominated American perfume industry. There were no rules for me to follow, no boundaries to fence me in. I made it up as I went along. The elephant in the room was the immutable fact that most American women only wore perfume on special occasions. No one knew why, and neither did I. It never occurred to me not to wear scent (still true).

I jumped into the breach and began what turned out to be a forty-year joyride (speed bumps, road blocks, potholes, and all) through the worlds of fashion, theater, movies, art, education, science, TV, and the business of fragrance. I gave free rein to my passion for perfume and fought against and prevailed over every windmill I encountered. How thrilling it was for me and my supporters to find that our untiring efforts ultimately allowed the Fragrance Foundation to create the environment for the small fragrance industry to grow big enough and strong enough to take on the world.

Along the way, I found myself in the surprising position of witness and game changer for women in and out of the industry. I involved myself in a wide variety of activities that I hoped would broaden the industry's reach and encourage its long-term support. Much of what I accomplished was because I looked outside the fragrance industry to make connections with unlikely partners in far-flung fields for inspiration and cooperation. I reached out to a broad swath of newsmakers: educators, historians, designers, performers, futurists, and social and sensory scientists who potentially could bring the power and relevance of their accomplishments to what I considered a too-insular industry. It took quite a bit of doing, but I am here to report, as you will see, that eventually all of the pieces did come together to help build the Fragrance Foundation (and the industry) into an international force.

It took me ten years to bring the foundation back to life. I can honestly say I had no idea how difficult it would be. I mistakenly thought time was on my side and with some good public relations, the tide would turn. Wrong! The reality was that I found myself responsible for a very weak and defenseless infant that practically no one really wanted to save. I was reminded on more than one occasion, "Annette, no one wants or needs the Fragrance Foundation. Forget it."

Despite the discouraging words, I was energized by the challenge and what turned out to be a labor of love. Hand-holding was out. I had to step up unimpeded and vigorously nurture this abandoned baby. It was an exercise in beating the odds. For reasons I can't possibly explain, I never lost faith, and revive the foundation I did. The slow-growth industry, however, was still unimpressed and reluctant to reevaluate its support. Anyway, the industry was still unclear about whether or not such an organization had any relevance.

While they were figuring it out, I began to strategize how I could speed up the process and what steps I would have to take, immediately, to move forward with a dramatically different and visionary agenda to capture the attention of the powers at the top. Much to everyone's surprise (including my own), that is exactly what happened. I pursued what many believed was an impossible dream. In fact, it did take those ten years of mostly unappreciated dedication to accomplish this metamorphosis. I realized that I better go all-out to reach industry leaders in the hope of rallying their support.

The perfect person to begin with, I felt, was a dashing Frenchman, Edouard Cournand, who had been a decorated fighter pilot in World War I. At that time, he was president of one of the most important French fragrance companies, Lanvin, whose famous ad line, "Promise her anything, but give her Arpege," is still remembered by fragrance aficionados. His office was in the elegant Savoy Plaza Hotel (now the site of the General Motors Building) on Fifth Avenue. It was almost a mirror image of the Plaza Hotel across the street. Lanvin maintained an exclusive perfume boutique on the promenade-street level of the hotel. Each night, the brilliantly lit glass walls of the shop revealed a mannequin dressed as a French maid wearing an elegant black-and-white uniform. On her head, a perky matching cap. Around her waist, an embroidered white apron with a big bow in the back. She always held a large feather duster. The "maid" was placed in different and sometimes impertinent poses and situations each night, which really had nothing to do with cleaning or perfume. She danced (with her feather-duster partner), read racy novels, and gossiped on her French phone with her feet resting on one of the perfume counters. She became a must-see not only for industry members but for Fifth Avenue strollers to discover what the Lanvin maid was up to. It was great fun!

I began a campaign of daily telephone calls to Mr. Cournand. His secretary, however, blocked my efforts. I had just about given up when an unexpected opportunity presented itself. Another client of mine, William Randall, president of Sea and Ski suntan products, was in New York from California, and we were set to meet on Saint Patrick's Day. Luckily for me, he was staying at the Savoy Plaza. I was to join him in his suite in the early afternoon. I made my way through the parade, and when I reached the hotel, I decided to buy him a green carnation in the hotel's posh flower shop. While I was checking out the assortment, I saw Mr. Cournand shopping for flowers too. As he liked to remind me, I followed him from the roses to the gladiolas to the daffodils, whispering in his ear about how much I would like to meet and tell him about what was happening at the Fragrance Foundation. Finally, he threw up his arms in surrender when we reached the orchids. "Okay! Okay! Call my secretary tomorrow, and she will set an appointment." It was the break I was looking for. Of course, I did call, and this time I got through. After spending about twenty minutes or so with Mr. Cournand, explaining what we were hoping to do to resurrect the foundation and its potential importance to the industry, he agreed Lanvin would become a member.

What a coup. It opened the doors for me to call other movers and shakers in the fragrance industry. One by one, they joined, as well. There were, however, a couple of critical holdouts: Estée Lauder and Revlon. For a very long time (years, in fact) I was unable to convince them that supporting the Fragrance Foundation was an important business decision. I eventually did welcome Estée Lauder, with the help of the remarkable Rebecca McGreevey, vice president of public relations, who was eager to interact with the foundation. In the eighties, I pursued Paul Woolard, president of Revlon, until he invited me to lunch in his elegant wood-paneled offices. Although I wasn't sure if the meeting was successful, when we finished (interrupted, I might add, by endless telephone calls), he agreed to have the company join the foundation. I was on cloud nine.

In the late sixties, an unforeseen and most fortuitous turn of events changed everyone's game plan. Major pharmaceutical companies began to buy the distribution rights to the French perfume houses. Squibb bought Lanvin and later acquired Charles of the Ritz and YSL; Pfizer bought Coty; and American Cyanamid became the proud parent of Nina Ricci.

It was quickly apparent to me that these companies would welcome in-depth information about the industry in the United States. What an opportunity! I jumped into the void and began to publish materials identifying each of the companies on the market, their fragrance lines, where they were sold, and whatever other pertinent information I felt would be helpful. Slowly, very slowly, the growing industry began to turn to the foundation as a source.

I took advantage of the information gap by scheduling seminars with marketing and sales experts, and publishing newsletters and sales training materials for behind-the-counter personnel. I continually met with the industry's leaders to get their insights and advice. I began to push and push for participation and support over the next ten years. I have to admit it was a struggle. Critics used to claim there were more people on the dais than in the audience at my seminars. They were close to right. Nevertheless, I persevered and finally figured out how to expand attendance by providing the industry with the kind of cutting-edge, celebrity-laced insights they could embrace. Remember, this was all happening pre-internet. Obtaining and disseminating information in a timely and meaningful time frame was extremely difficult. I developed a series of seminars that more than met the needs and resulted in increasing support for the foundation. Two of the biggest successes were the annual December and January seminars: State of the Industry and Retailers' Review of Xmas Past. We invited major figures from the financial world for the first and a group of America's most important and influential retailers for the second. Each ensured packed houses.

Left to right, Leonard Stoller, Editor of the Givaudan Newsletter, Hazel Bishop, renowned cosmetic entrepreneur and financial analyst, and me.

On a cold January day in 1981, the Fragrance Foundation was holding its Retailers' Review of Xmas Past luncheon seminar in the Terrace Room of the Plaza in New York. Minutes before the program was set to begin, a member of my staff approached me on the dais with important news. When I heard what it was, I immediately stood up and tapped the microphone to get everyone's attention. "Please stand and join me in a toast." I have to say there was a quizzical, bemused response, but almost everyone did stand with glass in hand. "I have just been told Iran has released all the American hostages. Let's toast their return." Full-throated cheers filled the ballroom.

New Voices

I soon realized that the industry also needed to hear from outside experts who would provide insights into changes taking place around the world. One of my favorite go-to speakers was the futurist Edie Weiner, who shared her brilliant observations and predictions on many occasions. Others included authorities on globalization, the environment, ethnicity, psychology, and anthropology.

In the seventies, the great anthropologist and historian Margaret Mead accepted my invitation to address a meeting of the Fragrance Foundation. She arrived at the Plaza, with her famous six-foot-tall carved wooden staff in hand, to share her discoveries about the importance of the sense of smell and aromas in primitive cultures. Of course, her comments were fascinating, including her observation that "you can never have a personal relationship with someone whose smell you do not like."

After the meeting, she talked with many of the attendees and confided to me, "I think the trouble with your industry is that it thinks it is selling product, when in reality it is selling people."

I shared this profound observation with members of the fragrance industry whenever possible over the years.

Times A-Changing

As I've described, one of the main stumbling blocks the industry faced was that women in our part of the world did not use fragrance, except on special occasions. A dab of expensive perfume behind the ears and at the base of the throat was about it. Women usually only thought about wearing perfume when they stepped out on Saturday nights in their little black dresses accessorized by strings of pearls. Perfume was a status symbol usually considered the perfect luxury gift for a man to give to a woman.

In 1953, Estée Lauder, a relative newcomer in the industry, did an end run around the "perfume-only" establishment with an olfactory surprise: Youth Dew. She promoted it as a scented bath oil that doubled as perfume and proclaimed it "the sexiest fragrance ever." A dramatic, long-lasting oriental, Youth Dew—now available in many forms, including spray perfume—was priced well below most perfumes on the market at that time. It was an immediate hit and set the scene for the democratization of fragrance.

Few in or out of the industry were aware of a surprising street trend gaining popularity with hippies across the country. Determined to find a way to cover the smell of pot, they were elevating musk from perfume ingredient to a fragrance in its own right. The underground movement was totally out of sight of the industry. Unexpectedly, I had a front-row seat to what was happening. A company called Sunshine Natural Products, located in San Rafael, California, was looking for a public relations company, and someone recommended my agency. Sunshine was the brainchild of two tuned-in young entrepreneurs, Nick Poulos and his chemist friend Randy Kay. They invited me to visit their offices on the West Coast. I discovered the story behind what was beginning to be called the "musk revolution." At first they worked in a one-room lab. The over-the-top olfactory impact of their musk, which masked the smell of pot, created a demand from head shops across the country. It inspired friends of the soon-to-be fragrance revolutionaries to rent an old-school bus, dismantle its interior, and fill it with hundreds of bottles of musk oil. They drove it cross-country, selling the oils to enthusiastic head shops. A sky's-the-limit demand followed. Sunshine Natural Products was born.

To maintain its new and successful business the entrepreneurs hired a handful of young men and women who came down from the hills every morning, dressed in jeans and head scarves tied pirate-style. Several brought their German shepherds. It was quite a sight as they spent the day filling small bottles with musk oil in a large warehouse-type space. A few years later, Sunshine employed thirty people and had the capacity to bottle $333,333,333 worth of essence oils and body oils per month on a single-shift basis. In no time, the company added patchouli which, together with musk, captured a big and growing market of the young and restless. News of the "revolution" began to reach noses in the industry.

Bernie Mitchell, the dynamic president of Jovan, a newly formed Chicago-based company, and his partners, Barry Shipp and Dick Meyer, were among the first to pick up the scent. By 1972, working with one of the small suppliers in the industry, Elias Fragrances, the company introduced its own potent Musk Cologne for Women. It was an overnight success for grown-ups, as well as their children. Magazines and newspapers in the cities across America took notice and headlined the trend. The success of musk brought the fragrance industry down to earth with a bang. It was the first time in its history that what was happening on the street was giving top-of-the-line luxury fragrances a run for their money. Jovan followed up by introducing a series of fragrances popular with emerging young consumers, including patchouli. Eventually, an increasing number of companies took note and began to introduce street-smart fragrances that appealed to and could be afforded by a new generation of fragrance devotees. As his market grew, Bernie Mitchell reached out to me and without a moment's hesitation joined the Fragrance Foundation. It helped move his company into the mainstream. Helped us, too.

Barry Shipp, Executive Vice-President of Jovan and I having a chat.

Working the Women

By the mid-sixties, perfume-wearing patterns in the United States were about to be affected by the opening up of the job market to women.

In 1965, Coty, a conservative fragrance house that had been acquired by Pfizer, went all out to capitalize on the emerging trend with the launch of Imprévu (Unforeseen), its first new fragrance in twenty-five years. A woodsy floral chypre, it hit the American market with unusual flourish and flair. Major advertisements touting the news that "Imprévu is here" appeared in leading magazines from *McCall's* to *LIFE*. Coty was the first to run an ad in 1967 that included a scratch-and-sniff microencapsulation of the fragrance developed by the 3M Company. All a woman had to do was pop open a specially treated flap that was part of the ad and scratch the surface with her fingernail, and the fragrance was released for her to smell. Coty expanded the advertising theme by placing colorful banners on the sides of New York City buses. They created quite a buzz. So did a song Coty commissioned for the introduction of the fragrance. But by the eighties, Imprévu was a distant memory, as many competitive brands saturated the marketplace.

Revlon made its own mark in the burgeoning career-girl marketplace with its launch of Charlie in 1973. A fragrance with a man's name? Unheard of! Inexpensive, with bright, light-green notes and a floral heart, it could be worn to work and wherever else a savvy girl might find herself. The ad featured a smart-looking young woman striding across the page in, of all things, a pantsuit. As an aside, Charles Revson did not allow his women staff members to wear pants in the office—at least not at first.

Career women of all ages fell in love with Charlie. So did mothers, including mine. It became a blockbuster and inspired a whole new genre of fragrance. I can't begin to tell you how many "parents" have claimed Charlie as their own baby over the years, but true parentage will always be traced to the DNA of Charles Revson.

As the market became more hospitable, the industry began to burst at the seams. New fragrances, new concepts began to flood the market. Consumers were entranced.

Giorgio of Beverly Hills broke the mold in 1981. A year or so before, I was invited to a breakfast meeting with Gale and Fred Hayman, owners of the famous Rodeo Drive boutique in Beverly Hills, and their two marketing geniuses, Jim Roth and David Horner. The group was eager for me to smell several versions of the fragrance they were working on. About eight test bottles were lined up on the table. I sniffed each one and picked the scent that most appealed to me. I never knew if I had chosen the scent that finally came to market, but that didn't matter. It was a sensation. And for reasons known only to the olfactory gods, with very little promotion in the early days, it had a "catnip" effect on the consumer. Packaged in its bright yellow-and-white awning-style box, Giorgio became a symbol of the over-the-top lifestyle of the eighties, which also was being influenced by leading fashion designers, who found profits and even more prestige by lending their names to the most luxurious and original fragrances.[2]

Giorgio was the first to utilize the latest development in scent-strip technology by Arcade in its print magazine ad campaign. Unlike the earlier versions, which involved scratching the page with your nail to release the fragrance (which women didn't like to do), the new and improved fold at the outer edge of the ad page merely had to be lifted up to allow a consumer to smell the encapsulated fragrance on the paper or smooth it directly on her (or his) skin. An overwhelming response placed the scent strip on a fast track to becoming an irresistible marketing tool for the whole industry. Perfect for sampling a fragrance, it allowed consumers to sniff and evaluate a scent wherever and whenever. The scent strip (until it became smell-proof) was not appreciated by those who objected to smelling fragrance in their magazines.[3]

Unlike classic perfume construction, Giorgio's fantasy floral/oriental blend did not wait to develop in stages. The company claimed it burst out of the bottle fully developed. I remember standing in the Perfume Department of Macy's in New York, watching young models dressed in yellow-and-white-striped sweaters to match the perfume's packaging. They stood in the aisle in front of the counter, spraying the scent. Customers walked past, smelled the fragrance in the air, turned around, and without a moment's hesitation bought a bottle. For several years, it was the biggest selling fragrance in the industry, ever. On the downside, an anti-Giorgio trend emerged, particularly in some restaurants, which banned customers who were wearing the fragrance. It was the subject du jour for the rumor mill, despite the fact that Giorgio was certainly not the only strong fragrance on the market. I always wondered if it wasn't a public relations ploy by anxious competitors.

Later in the decade, Calvin Klein made headlines with the introduction of his unisex fragrance, CK One. A light, bright citrus, it was created to appeal to the growing army of young men and women who, like the hippies in the sixties, were totally comfortable wearing similar clothes (especially jeans) and wearing their hair long and flowing. Under the baton of the brilliant Robin Burns, it quickly turned into a youthquake that transformed the selling and wearing of fragrance (and, I might add, fashion too). The company set up displays and sold CK One in men's clothing stores, music outlets, and bookstores, as well as in traditional venues. It was the rage in those transitional years when, slowly but surely, the widening fashion and fragrance differences between the sexes were melting away.

Despite all these new entries, a reality check revealed the great classics like Chanel No. 5, Miss Dior, Shalimar, and L'Air du Temps still retained their universal appeal.

Keeping track of fragrances past and present became a major and often inaccurate undertaking. Michael Edwards changed all that. Over thirty years ago, I had the privilege of meeting this erudite and remarkable Brit. He was eager for an exchange of ideas about what would become his masterwork, *Fragrances of the World*. We found a cozy spot at the Museum of Modern Art and talked and talked for hours. In 2014, he celebrated the thirtieth anniversary of what has become an industry bible, listing over seven thousand fragrances. Elegant full-color, hardcover volumes are updated and published annually. Michael has also developed a fragrance database that provides an easy-to-access method to assure the accuracy of each fragrance description and allows for sorting and cross-referencing more than sixteen thousand fragrances in all retail categories. He received two FiFi Awards for his efforts. I have noted many times that Michael's remarkable contributions will serve the industry for generations to come.

At a recent Fragrance Plume Awards ceremony, he surprised everyone by announcing his latest book, featuring America's greatest fragrances, will be published in 2018 and dedicated to the extraordinary Evelyn Lauder—and me. What a thrilling moment!

As the fragrance category became more mainstream, I was pushing behind the scenes for the industry to put more emphasis on fragrance in all its many forms, not only perfume. My goal was to change focus and give greater importance to more affordable eau de parfums, toilet waters, and colognes that women could buy for themselves. In fact, eau de parfum was destined to become a consumer favorite. It has been described by industry watchers as more bang for the buck.

I continued to encourage women to build wardrobes of fragrance, campaigning tirelessly to help them understand that one fragrance doesn't work in every situation. Rather—like fashion, I stressed to whoever would listen—fragrance should be worn to enhance different occasions and seasons. At first I was met with a lot of resistance. Many women still wanted to be recognized by the one fragrance they chose as their signature scent, if they wore one at all. Once they became part of America's workforce, however, they were more open to the multifaceted roles of fragrance, as well as fashion. Today, having a wardrobe of fragrance—for work, play, romance, sexual allure—is basic for women and men too. True, there are still some who cling to one fragrance no matter how attitudes have changed, but they are in the minority.

From a business perceptive, when women embraced the "wardrobe of fragrance" concept, it gave companies the opportunity to ratchet up the number of fragrances they could create and launch on a regular basis.

Richard Solomon, President of Parfums Lanvin
with Vogue editor-in-chief Diana Vreeland.

Until the seventies, most fragrance companies depended on a lead scent, and years could go by before another was introduced. Usually, their second and third fragrances were not heavily promoted, so they never became stars. Instead, they were destined to orbit around the formidable number one. No wonder the industry was so small. But it definitely was not going to stay that way.

The groundwork we had laid for the organization and the industry was beginning to pay off. In the early seventies, estimated fragrance sales at retail were approximately $300 million for women and $155 million for men. Big changes were in the offing, and the fragrance market was set to explode. With a very small and dedicated staff (six of us in all, plus my mother, whose services were "free for a cup of tea"), Annette Green Associates, on behalf of the Fragrance Foundation, took on fragrance and its world with gusto!

To get a sense of what happened and how, I have scattered clues everywhere. They are not meant as a ten-steps-to-success formula, but rather to provide insights into what it took a real person (me) to break through the clutter, the competition, and the naysayers, and have fun along the way. My hope is that as a contemporary can-do spirit, you will find strategies that are translatable and applicable to twenty-first-century entrepreneurial yearnings. They can make it possible to defy time and circumstance, even in our technological, self-absorbed society. The constants are laser-like focus and loving to live with a 24/7 obsession, no matter how the world changes. Each of my tales could be considered "case histories" or pieces in a jigsaw puzzle. Put them all together, and they will reveal a treasure trove of techniques that allowed me to tame an unexplored landscape. Best of all, from a creative perspective, this is a landscape that can be reimagined to suit a variety of purposes and even jolt dormant creative urges into action.

I hope, too, that as you follow your dreams, you will reject the alternate truth that falsely claims creativity in the workplace is dead. Despite rumors to the contrary, imagination is still the coin of the realm (always has been, always will be!). In fact, the closer we get to the mastery of creative thinking, the faster we will find ourselves in a boredom-free safe zone where the threat of being replaced by a robot is practically nil. Don't laugh. Thousands of people already have been, and many more will be. Nevertheless, in my long life (ninety-three years at this writing), I can attest it is possible to make oneself virtually fireproof by embracing an illuminating life of creativity, imagination, and inspiration. Thank goodness, there is still no machine that can duplicate these ideal states of being. What's more, experiential clues can trigger a successful mindset no matter who and where they come from. It doesn't matter whether your connection to fragrance is professional, personal, or nonexistent. There are gender-neutral universal truths that we all share: dedication, curiosity, courage, and of course, know-how. Success won't happen overnight. As I've said, it took ten years before I had a breakthrough.

Getting the industry's attention was no small feat. First I tried a series of seminars. Little response. I fretted about what to do next and decided to return to what had really worked when I was coming up through the ranks: the irresistibility of celebrities! Still, I needed a practical strategy. I found it, too, by imagining how to connect underappreciated women in the fragrance field with famous and admired women in the arts. I decided to honor illustrious women before a luncheon audience of the industry's VIPs. The theme I settled on was "Give Thanks for Women," and the timing each year was the Thursday before Thanksgiving.

I turned to the British actress Hermione Gingold (think the movie *Gigi*) for advice. I had met her in the early seventies through a tough, no-holds-barred London theater agent, Viola Rubber.[4] How grateful I was to be for that introduction.

Our paths crossed many times, but never more dramatically than when I conceived the Give Thanks for Women luncheon. Miss Gingold wasn't able to participate at the time, but she guided me in reaching out to friends of hers who might participate. She was convinced, as was I, that these luncheons would encourage the industry to focus more intensely on the increasingly important roles women were beginning to play in every facet of society. In the fragrance industry, believe it or not, women had little status at the time. Few acknowledged the multifaceted lives women were actually beginning to lead. My hope in creating the luncheon was that there would be a subliminal rub-off on the power structure, which would end up being a wake-up call rewarding talented women as professional colleagues. In the context of today's world, that may seem absurd, but back in the day, the industry had a very laissez-faire attitude about women as executives. They filled the secretarial pools, worked behind the counters of department stores and drugstores, and handled press relations, but unless your name was on the building

(Helena Rubinstein, Elizabeth Arden, and Estée Lauder), chances of reaching the executive suite were very slim indeed.

Colleen Dewhurst with her husband, George Scott captivated the audience while my collegues and I enjoyd their charming repartee.

From its inception, the luncheon had been an industry hit. I leaned on everybody I knew (or had met over the years), in or out of show business, to help me reach the most accomplished, newsworthy celebrities. We asked the guests of honor to speak about their careers with emphasis on the role sensory awareness and fragrance played in their lives and work. Each celebrity was presented with an inscribed crystal perfume decanter designed by Verreries Brosse, creators of crystalline perfume bottles, in appreciation of their attendance.

The presence of these remarkably successful women was bait to bring out top brass. And what a roster we had: my all-time favorite movie idol, Bette Davis, revered author Fannie Hurst, British comedian and actress Bea Lillie, and the glamorous stage star Colleen Dewhurst. She arrived with her then husband, actor George C. Scott, who announced to the audience that he had "no idea why" he was there. Neither, I have to admit, did I. And then there was the Hungarian glamour girl, actress, and much-married Zsa Zsa Gabor. In her inimitable style, she set off a ripple of laughter at one of the luncheons when she closed her remarks with a not-so-subtle sign-off, "Zsa Zsa calling." She obviously thought it would inspire the attendees from Avon. It didn't.

No laughing matter, however, was the bill she ran up with the limousine service I had arranged to escort her. Instead of going from the luncheon back to her hotel, she began a round of shopping throughout Manhattan that took her well into the early evening. Of course, I had no idea until I received the invoice, which certainly broke the budget. Still, the glamorous Zsa Zsa lit up the luncheon with her legendary beauty and Hungarian charm. Obviously, that comes with a cost.

Zza Gabor joins me for a post luncheon photo before her shopping spree.

My earlier contact with Pearl Bailey allowed me to reach out to her with an invitation for her to be one of our guests of honor. She was very much in the news at that time as a star of the all-black cast in *Hello, Dolly!* She agreed to be honored but at the last minute became ill. As it turned out, her understudy, Thelma Carpenter, offered to stand in for Ms. Bailey. I hadn't realized at that time that she hadn't asked for permission. Nevertheless, she was a lovely guest, and everyone enjoyed her remarks. I learned a month or two later from my mother, who happened to be strolling at Central Park and saw Ms. Bailey. She stopped to tell her how much the audience at our luncheon had appreciated Ms. Carpenter. In no uncertain terms, the diva advised my mother that her understudy's appearance did not please her and had not been approved by her. So much for off-stage charm!

Each year, the pressure was on to rally famous stars to be our guests of honor, and an invitation went out once more to Hermione Gingold. This time, she accepted. But several days before the luncheon, she called from London full of apologies that she wouldn't be back on time. I tried everything in my playbook to encourage her to reverse this bad news. She just couldn't. Finally, in desperation, I asked her if it would be possible to contact one of her friends in New York to take her place. "I'll try," she promised.

The next day she called. "How would you feel about Julie Andrews?"

You can imagine my reaction. The thought of having the sensational star of the blockbuster hit *My Fair Lady* took my breath away. I didn't tell anyone. The day of the luncheon, I stood at the mike and reported, "Hermione Gingold is in London and sends her regrets."

There was total silence in the ballroom of the Pierre Hotel, where the luncheon was being held that year. After a pause, I continued, "However, Miss Gingold has asked her friend Julie Andrews to stand in for her, and she accepted. May I present her to you now."

An audible gasp greeted Miss Andrew's arrival on stage, and the loudest and longest applause followed. What a delicious moment that was!

We ended the series on another high note in the winter of 1986.[5] A sellout crowd gathered at the Plaza in New York to celebrate. The focus of the attendees' admiration was the great operatic diva Jessye Norman. She spoke movingly about her thrilling and challenging career journey, as did the fabulous stage-and-nightclub performer Elaine Stritch, film-and-theater critic Pia Lindstrom, and best-selling author Shana Alexander, who all shared the inspirational stories of their lives and drives. We had invited the legendary French entrepreneur, singer, and actress, Regine, but because she was detained in Paris, her sister appeared in her place and spoke charmingly about the voluptuous world Regine had created here and abroad.

Jessye Norman greeting our longtime mutual friend,
Elsie Hirsch who made her appearance possible.

The elegant guests of honor certainly presaged many glamorous days and starry nights to come that would lift the Fragrance Foundation and its members into the stratosphere.

---

1. The Toilet Goods Association became the Cosmetic, Toiletry, and Fragrance Association and is currently known as the Personal Care Products Council, or PCPC.
2. Calvin Klein, Carolina Herrera, Givenchy, Jean Paul Gaultier, Halston, Donna Karan, Ralph Lauren, Oscar de la Renta, Oleg Cassini, Yves Saint Laurent, and Geoffrey Beene. In 1968, Norman Norell was heralded as the first American designer to lend his name to a perfume (Revlon acquired the brand three years later). A national advertising campaign proclaimed it "the first great perfume born in America." A luxurious green floral, it was a runaway success with women executives from coast to coast. They not only wore the perfume but they kept the inkwell-inspired, square-cut crystal bottle in full view on their desks. It became a talisman of their status. A new interpretation of the Norell fragrance was introduced for Christmas 2015, courtesy of Parlux. In addition, a contemporary bottle reminiscent of the original, a limited edition was offered in Baccarat handblown crystal flacons. An ad campaign touted the scent as "an American classic fragrance remastered."

3. Jokesters had their day. The fun of it all was captured in the *New Yorker Book of Cartoons*, which the magazine published through its division the Cartoon Bank, to celebrate the Fragrance Foundation's 2004 FiFi Awards (chapter 4). The cartoonist, Liza Donnelly, pictured a man and a woman seated near each other in a waiting room at an airport. The copy line read, "Is that you who smells so great, or your magazine?" All attendees of the ceremony received the delightful eighty-six-page book of amusing perfume cartoons that had appeared in the magazine over the years. It was underwritten by Luxe Pack New York, one of the sponsors of the awards ceremony that year.

4. I had the good fortune to meet Viola Rubber in the late fifties when I was public relations director at Lentheric and she was stage manager of the Broadway play *Two's Company* starring Bette Davis. Viola had approached me about the possibility of providing makeup for the show. Without a moment's hesitation, I agreed. I jumped at the opportunity to meet the star, whom I had long admired. When the day came to take publicity pictures with Miss Davis, we all gathered backstage in her dressing room. It was filled with press agents, personal dressers, and representatives of the show. I mentioned to her that I would be grateful to have a picture taken with her. At the end of the session, one of the show's representatives announced it was time to leave so that Miss Davis could prepare for the matinee. To everyone's surprise (including my own), she turned and announced, "I would like to have my picture taken with Miss Green." I was thrilled by her magnanimous gesture. Long story short, she and I became friends. We learned we were both born under the sign of Taurus and came to share an appreciation of each other, which I have treasured all these years.

5. On a nostalgic note for those readers from the fragrance industry who may have attended the last Give Thanks for Women luncheon celebration, the presenters at the time included Philip Miller, William Rubin, Lawrence Wechsler, James Bosek, Burton Tansky, and Robert Miller.

II

Promenade Provocateur

You must have scent for them, and a scent is like a sixth sense which combines hearing, seeing, and smelling.

—Jules Verne
Around the World in Eighty Days

One of the facts I had to face as I geared up to expand the visibility of fragrance was its inherent invisibility. It always took a backseat to the "eye candy" of fashion. Editorially, if fragrance was mentioned at all, it was with an off-the-cuff credit inside a short caption describing a dress, suit, or coat: "The model is wearing such-and-such perfume." I decided to try to change the dynamics by uniting the two in the Fashion/Fragrance Promenade.

Member companies were invited to interpret their famous fragrances in costumes to be modeled and judged at a gala at the Waldorf Astoria. Promenade judges included the renowned fashion columnist Eugenia Sheppard. Twelve companies enthusiastically signed up and turned their creative people loose to develop what they hoped would be winning designs that emphasized the relationship of fragrance to fashion. All the models promenaded together in a grand finale

In the sixties, the creator of unabashedly romantic fashions, Oscar de la Renta,[1] was a relatively unknown designer working for Elizabeth Arden. She chose Oscar to create a costume to express her classic fragrance, Blue Grass. He turned out to be the lynchpin of the Promenade.

When the big night came, I placed the judges at a table in the center of the ballroom floor for easy viewing of each costumed model as she appeared on stage and then circled the ballroom. Oscar's model was the dramatic six-foot-tall Veruschka. She wore a nude bodysuit wrapped in clear cellophane. Veruschka waved a wand (well before the invention of the aerosol) that magically released the fragrance as she glided around the ballroom floor. It made a terrific impression. I never did find out how Oscar did it, but he walked away with first prize. Miss Arden was impressed. Oscar kidded me whenever we met over the years. "Annette, you made me."

Several other contenders were also winners. Henri Bendel, which at that time was located in its fabulous art deco building on West Fifty-Seventh Street, decided to showcase its Beauty Department, the Bird Cage. The entry turned out to be a massive golden birdcage. When it was rolled out on the stage, a glamorous model, bedecked in brilliantly colored feathers, created a sensation as she happily swung back and forth on her perch. (Years later, Chanel created a look-alike in a commercial also featuring a girl in a golden cage. Made me wonder if someone at Chanel's ad agency had come across old coverage of the Promenade.)

Another winner was International Flavors & Fragrances, one of the industry's leading fragrance suppliers. When their model, wearing a slim, floor-length white gown, reached center stage, she pulled hidden strings, and suddenly the gown billowed into a glorious antebellum creation covered with fresh flowers.

Because the Promenade received overwhelming praise and attendance, the board decided to do it again the following year. There was even some thought about making it a national effort. Once again, Oscar wowed the crowd. A major hitch developed, however, involving George Barrie, president of Fabergé (one of America's leading fragrance houses in those years.) The company decided to build a larger-than-life version of its bright-yellow powder box from a new Kiku bath collection conceived by the brilliant creative director of the company, Amelia Bassin. A supersize reproduction of the yellow ball was carried onto the ballroom floor. It sat securely atop two broad poles, which in turn rested on the shoulders of four scantily clad "out of Africa" male models. When the men and their cargo reached the center of the ballroom floor, the cover of the ball was lifted and, to everyone's surprise, out popped George Barrie's third and then current wife, Gloria Barrie.

Competition among the companies was intense. Winning was a serious, expensive, and egocentric matter. When Kiku didn't win, Mr. Barrie was definitely not happy. What I hadn't anticipated was that I would be the object of his anger. As I walked across the ballroom floor at the conclusion of the evening, I was startled to feel a strong fist in the small of my back, perfectly positioned to give me quite a shove. I wheeled around to see who the culprit was and was more than a little startled to find Mr. Barrie scowling at me. After I made it abundantly clear I did not appreciate either his fist in my back or the anticipated shove, he quickly disappeared into the crowd.

After some serious Monday morning quarterbacking with my staff and the board, everyone agreed that, despite the great success of the Fragrance/Fashion Promenade, it had the ingredients of becoming too controversial. A reality check reminded one and all—especially me—that when push came to shove, the negatives of high costs and loss of face by the nonwinners outweighed the positives. I went back to the proverbial drawing board. Little did any of us know that the industry's biggest game changer—the FiFi Awards—was waiting in the wings.

---

1. I had the privilege of sharing the spotlight with Oscar de la Renta on and off throughout the years. In fact, we were both honored by Lighthouse International, a renowned New York–based charity dedicated to improving the lives of the vision impaired, at the annual "Winternight" 1997 benefit gala. The evening raised over $1.2 million.

The Game Changer

Favorite Co-conspirators

Geoffrey Webster, president, worldwide Roure
John Ledes, publisher, Beauty Fashion
James Preston, chairman and CEO, Avon
Sally Yeh, president, Bijan Fragrances
Dr. Fernando Aleu, president of the Fragrance Foundation, president of Puig of Barcelona, and associate professor of neuropathology, New York University College of Medicine in New York
Jean Claude Moreau, president, Pochet of America
Robert Miller, executive vice president of the Fragrance Foundation and president and CEO of Charles of the Ritz Group
Eugene Milano, president of Dana Perfumes and a member of the board of the Fragrance Foundation
Davie Lerner, Stage designer
Kitty D'Alessio, president of Chanel, vice president of the Fragrance Foundation board
Elliot Stone, president of the Boston department store Jordan Marsh
Milton Stern, founder and chairman of Parfums Stern
Charles Miller-Smith, chairman of PPF International
Marty Bloom, president of May Merchandising Corporation
Enrique Puig, Antonio Puig, SA
Alex Ventos, general manager, Firmenich Fine Fragrances, SA
Jaime Pla, Interlain Cosmeticos, SA
Antonio Bergilos, Ventas de Perfumeria y Cosmetica
Walter Hinrichs, president of the Fragrance Foundation Deutschland and general manager of Estée Lauder Companies, Germany

Reinhard-Dieter Wolf, president of the European Federation of Perfumery Retailers and president of the German Federation of Perfumery

I like things to happen; and if they don't happen, I like to make them happen.

— **Winston Churchill**

f the fascinations of fame, glamour, and theatrical hijinks tickle your fancy, imagine the impact on the fragrance world when the glorious superstars (think Elizabeth Taylor, Catherine Deneuve, and Sophia Loren) took center stage in the mid-eighties. Each had a namesake fragrance on her mind. They were, however, outliers. Fashion designers ruled. Few fragrances linked to movie stars had ever gained traction with the public.[1] No one really understood why. It could have been the stars themselves, who never seemed to leave the screen for the real world. Yet the age of celebrity fragrances was in lift-off mode, so their timing was perfect. Most importantly, the creation of the stupendously successful FiFi Awards ceremony a decade earlier provided the perfect stage for celebrity strutting and paparazzi hullabaloo.

The spark for what was to become an international industry game changer caught fire on that lovely Parisian evening I told you about as I sipped my wine and pondered the foundation's future. Like the proverbial bolt out of the blue, it was suddenly obvious that the natural next step was to create a strategy for honoring the best of the best each year with awards in the mode of the movie world's Oscars and Broadway's Tonys. I began to block out my vision of what such a concept might look like. By the time the evening ended, I was on an emotional high that lasted until my return to New York the following day.

The first thing I did was visit with a friend who knew the behind-the-scenes workings of the Tony Awards. I was anxious for his opinion of my plan. He was more than encouraging and urged me on. Next, I met with the late Irwin Alfin. In addition to being the president of Chanel at that time, he was also president of the Fragrance Foundation. Irwin was enthusiastic about the proposal and confident that the concept was so powerful there would be no problem getting the approval of the board. He was right.

Once I had the green light, I didn't waste any time developing the ceremony. The plan was to present what were to be called the Fragrance Foundation Recognition Awards. Winners would be chosen by the industry. (It wasn't until the early eighties they were nicknamed FiFis by John Ledes, the influential publisher of two industry trade publications, *Beauty Fashion* and *Cosmetic World*. The nickname caught on and became the trademark for a worldwide celebration of fragrance excellence.)

Curtain Up

Originally dubbed the Gala Awards Dinner Dance, the first ceremonies took place in the ballroom of the Plaza in 1973 to honor 1972 introductions. There were just seven honorees based on industry voting:

1. Chanel No. 19: the most successful introduction of a new fragrance;
2. Norell from Revlon: the most exciting promotion;
3. Azuree from Estée Lauder: most exciting bath line;
4. Audace, Parfums Rochas: most appealing package introduction;
5. Chanel: most effective sales training;
6. Chanel: most effective national advertising; and
7. Cachet, Prince Matchabelli: most effective new product concept.

Award nominees and winners were projected on a single screen by two talents I had worked with on other projects: Sam Shadid (today, Sam is considered one of the stars of the advertising world) and John Frontino, Giovanni Design Associates. They were extremely creative and did a lot with very little.

For the first few years, winners received a framed eight-inch-square, colorful, abstract collage, designed by graphic artist Bill Goldberg. He intermingled calligraphy, art, metals, and paper to spell out each winner's name, awards category, and date of the ceremony. Leading magazine publishers and beauty editors presented the awards to the applause of approximately 250 industry attendees.

Tickets cost $50. Guests had to buy chits for drinks (which created a firestorm). The following year, we raised the prices and opened the bar. Happiness reigned.

The award that came to signify fragrance excellence was the work of the renowned French perfume bottle designer Pierre Dinand. Created in 1975, it combined two twelve-inch abstract crystal columns, produced in France by the perfume bottle manufacturer Pochet. My guide through the process was the ever-helpful charming president, Jean Claude Moreau. The crystal columns were meant to represent a man and a woman embracing a crystal droplet. Sadly, several years ago, the magnificent FiFi award was unceremoniously replaced by a glass slab. I shudder to think how the film industry would react if, suddenly, the famed Oscar statue morphed into a golden plate. I urged Donald Loftus, then chairman of the board, to encourage the board to reverse the decision to change the award. He tried, he told me, but to no avail. So now, nobody really knows what the FiFi actually looks like, and word is out that yet another design is in the offing. *Quel dommage!*

In the mid-seventies, designer Davie Lerner became my partner in stagecraft. Together, we conjured up the most extraordinary visual designs each year based on the themes I conceived for the ceremonies. One was based on a dream I had about a blue rose. He gave it his own imaginative twist by constructing a gigantic blue rose with three-dimensional rose petals surrounding a screen strategically placed at the heart of the rose. In the early eighties, we created a spectacular black-lacquered Busby Berkeley "stairway to the stars" stage design that gave nominees a dramatic setting for lounging, sitting, and standing. When the curtain opened, the audience was dazzled by the glamorous tableau.

Over the years we developed themes that were featured on stage and in the audio-visual presentations. Davie captured the fun and theatricality of the theme "That's Scentertainment" (coined by the incomparable Amelia Bassin) for our twenty-sixth annual awards ceremony. It inspired him to construct a set reminiscent of a movie marquee of the forties to capture the mood of Hollywood nostalgia. The set for the "Best of '93" took its inspiration from the world of music. Silver, gray, white, and black parachute silk banners spotlighted the FiFi logo and the theme "Music in the Air," and were framed by four towers of changing lights. At the twenty-fourth annual awards ceremonies, a comet soared across the set, sending the FiFi logo into space. On the screen, Star Wars technology introduced the 1995 finalists in a burst of nebulae. For the twenty-first birthday celebration of

the awards, Davie designed a fabulous metallic-gold-and-black stage set featuring a new FiFi logo (which he had redesigned) in a jewel-like setting.

After a couple of years, it became obvious it was time to glam up the proceedings with as many celebrities as possible. The timing was perfect because it coincided with a new fascination on the part of well-known personalities from the entertainment world in having fragrances created and named after them. I reached out to managers and public relations representatives of the celebrities and dangled the potential and real promise that participation of their famous clients would give them unprecedented visibility to the industry they were so eager to join. It worked! Legends from the worlds of theatre, film, fashion, opera, TV, dance, and literature made star turns as presenters of the awards each and every year. I can't imagine what we would have done without them—and in many cases, vice versa.

As the awards gained momentum, voting procedures and awards categories were dropped, added, and replaced to reflect the dynamism

Here I am making a challenging entrance.

Left to right, glamorous model Carmen, Broadway legend Carol Channing, forties movie star Claire Trevor, performer Billie Dee Williams, movie legends Arlene Dahl, Jane Powell, Joan Bennett and actor/tenor Allan Jones.

Sharing the spotlight with actress Isabella Rossellini.

of the growing industry and its changing priorities. There certainly was nothing static or sacrosanct about the categories. When I retired in 2003, the industry was celebrating winners in over twenty of them.

Indispensable Icons

By the time the second annual ceremonies were held, several new awards categories were added to the ballot: Advertising, Sales, Training, and Retailing. The board also agreed to add a Hall of Fame award to recognize the icons who influenced the remarkable growth of the industry in the United States. Election to receive this coveted honor was to be based on a unanimous vote by members of the board. The first recipient in 1974 was Estée Lauder. Her election set the stage for all the greats in the industry who followed, including Charles Revson in 1975. Two of the founders of the Fragrance Foundation, H. Gregory Thomas and Jean Desprez, were posthumously honored in 1976 and 1977, respectively. Hall of Famers were always saluted by the industry at the conclusion of the award ceremonies.

Each honoree was invited to select the person who would present the award. In 1996, when Jim Preston was elected, I visited with him in his office to share the news. He was truly moved. So was I, when he asked if I would do the honors. Jim and I had a long and meaningful relationship during the years he served as treasurer of the board. He was incredibly supportive and encouraging. Under his guidance, the Fragrance Foundation was always on solid financial footing.

Another standout moment was the year when the late, much-admired Geoffrey Webster was elected to the Hall of Fame. His presenter was Sally Yeh, who was not only a longtime colleague of Geoff's but a dear and treasured friend. Geoff cut an quite impressive figure that evening. He proudly wore the medals he had received as a Vietnam War hero in the US Air Force. Sally paid him an exquisite tribute. Many of us who were there still remember it:

> Geoffrey Webster is a brilliant executive, an accomplished artist, a seasoned aviator, and a military hero. As an officer in the army commanding a helicopter gunship operation, he received over forty medals and decorations during his tour of duty in Vietnam. I understand he still holds the record for flying the fastest helicopter rescue mission while under enemy fire.
>
> In January of this year, he decided to pursue his personal interests, including his childhood dream of flying solo across the country in his own airplane.
>
> He has served as a member of the board of directors of the Fragrance Foundation since 1990, and during his nine-year tenure, he was unquestionably one of the most supportive members. He and his company sponsored many activities, from special events during annual Fragrance Weeks to underwriting the opening of the Annette Green Museum, to which he donated the beautiful Erte sculpture, *Perfume*, now on display at the museum. Tonight he is receiving a very special award from the Fragrance Foundation, one that I know he will display proudly. For all the contributions he has made to the fragrance industry, for all he has done to further our mission and success, we now salute him.

Political Correctness

The awards also gave the foundation the opportunity to spotlight the pleasures of the fragrance experience to those who might not have found it relevant to their particular field. This was especially true of the fashion magazine editors. As I've said, they gave very little editorial credit to fragrances in the first half of the twentieth century. It inspired the board to add an award to honor the best fragrance coverage by a magazine. The payoff was big. Beauty editors began to devote major space to full-length articles on fragrances and the sense of smell (and still do.) Fragrances became an editorial "must" at holiday times and throughout the year. New fragrance introductions made news in every issue. Techniques of buying, wearing, and caring for fragrance became essential editorials.

A Moveable Feast

The FiFi Awards ceremonies were always hotel-based. As the audience grew, we moved from the Plaza to the grand ballroom of the Waldorf-Astoria, where we stayed for many years, except for two ceremonies held at the Sheraton Center and the New York Hilton. My office established sophisticated voting and judging procedures with the help of counsel. Our accounting firm received the ballots and tabulated them. I was the "chief cook and bottle washer." I wrote, produced, directed, and staged every ceremony. The icing on the cake, for me, was playing ringmaster. I guess the pleasure of being front and center before an appreciative audience was a left over from my youthful "Broadway baby" fantasies.[2]

Fortunately, the basics were backed up by an incredible team, led by my partner, Lois Berk, who were all devoted to making my yearly FiFi dreams a reality. Unexpected helping hands also made a quite a difference. Always indispensable to the success of the evening, as well as my peace of mind, was the office manager's husband, Vincent Gray, a banker in real life who arrived without fanfare to unpack the FiFi awards every year with the greatest aplomb and place them carefully in order of presentation on the winners' table.

An unprecedented New York City hotel strike in 1985 turned out to be a stroke of luck. It sent me on a wild chase to find a venue to stage the ceremony and have space for dinner too. I discovered Avery Fisher Hall at Lincoln Center was available. What a momentous change that turned out to be as we prepared to celebrate our thirteenth anniversary.

The magic began on a glorious spring evening. Cocktails were served around the reflecting pool, where the brilliant white Moore sculpture held sway. I remember standing at the glass wall on the second floor of Avery Fisher Hall and looking down at the crowd, feeling thrilled (and oddly surprised) that everything we had worked so hard to achieve was actually happening.

To alert everyone when the reception was over, I had arranged for a brass ensemble to appear at the pool and blow their horns with as much flourish as possible. They did, but no one made the slightest effort to leave. Finally, I had to move through the crowd myself and encourage them to come into the Hall so the ceremonies could begin. At last, they did, though reluctantly. They were having too much fun.

Two Forever Crystal fragrances (inspired by the TV hit *Dynasty*) were up for awards that evening. Thanks to Robert Miller, the charming and glamorous stars of the show—Linda Evans, Robert Stack, and John Forsythe—were among the presenters. Later, they collected FiFis for the fragrances that had won. Their appearance created a sensation.

Looking back reminded me that O. J. Simpson was also one of our presenters. Universally admired at that time as a TV star and football hero, he presented an award to Avon for its winning fragrance, Feraud Pour Homme. He was so handsome in his tux (I have a picture of us together to prove it) and gracious to one and all, who could have guessed how his future would turn out.

A gala dinner followed on the grand promenade at the Avery Fisher Hall. The next year, though, we were overwhelmed with attendees and had to make other arrangements. We left Lincoln Center for two years and held the awards at the New York Hilton and the Sheraton Center. We were, however, eager to return to Avery Fisher Hall. The caterers made it possible by proposing we rent the giant tent in nearby Damrosch Park for the dinner. We did, and it was perfect but needed a lot of decoration. Davie Lerner saved the day with the most dramatic and engaging lighting. Gramercy Park Flower Shop designed over-the-top decor for the tables. A long white canopy was constructed that led from the hall to the tent. After the ceremony ended, the glamorously gowned and tuxedoed crowd strolled under the canopy from one location to another. It was quite a sight.

The evening made such an impression that the foundation's usually superconservative special counsel, the late Arnold Burns (who later on

Christian Dior Perfumes, Inc.

212-759-1840

9 WEST 57TH STREET
NEW YORK, N.Y. 10019

June 6, 1985

Ms. Annette Green
The Fragrance Foundation
142 East 30 Street
New York, NY 10016

Dear Annette:

How did you do? Fantastically well!!

From a small ballroom at the Plaza to Avery Fischer Hall -- what
a road you have covered.

I bestow on you a special award -- that of High Priestess of the
Fragrance World with power of divination.

Congratulations on your great achievements.

Warmly,

Jean Pierre Lippmann
President

mwd

served as a top Justice Department official under President Reagan) presented me with a splendid seventeen-inch-high Lladró figure of Don Quixote, in tribute to impossible dreams. It still inspires me!

Star Turns

One of my favorite memories took place at the awards ceremony in 1981 when the voluptuous Sophia Loren accepted her FiFi for her first fragrance, Sophia, by Coty. The exquisite actress was wearing a black form-fitting gown with a very low décolleté. When Eugene Milano presented her with the FiFi, he gave her a congratulatory embrace that included resting his head on her famous bosom. It all took place in an instant. It was a funny, unscripted moment. I have often wondered whether Sophia was amused.

We reached another high note when Lena Horne agreed to be a presenter. Arriving for rehearsal for the fourteenth annual ceremonies, she threaded her way through the bare round dinner tables that filled the ballroom of the Waldorf Astoria. She was unrecognizable from afar. Her head was covered with a babushka, and she was wearing a rather nondescript dark jacket and trousers. No makeup, either. Of course, once she reached the stage and started to speak, there was no question who had arrived. Miss Horne agreed to participate thanks to Kitty D'Alessio, a longtime friend of Lena's. During the course of the rehearsal, Ms. Horne confided to me that she doubted whether an audience of fragrance executives would be very excited by her presence. She was not being disingenuous, either. I assured her that she couldn't be more wrong. When I introduced her on stage that evening, the entire audience of over a thousand stood, applauded, and cheered her. I could see she was taken aback, but very, very pleased. So was I.

The breathtakingly beautiful French film star Catherine Deneuve created quite a stir when she arrived for rehearsal. Waiting for her was the manager of the Waldorf, who was a bedazzled devotee. He dropped to his knees and begged her to move from her hotel to his. Unmoved by his plea, she almost brought him close to tears when she coolly advised him it was not possible. He left crestfallen. At the ceremony that evening, minutes before she was set to go on stage with her copresenter, Elliot Stone, Miss Deneuve suddenly expressed her reluctance to participate. After more than a bit of encouragement, she agreed—if all she had to do was open the envelope and Elliot Stone would announce the winner. But of course! All was forgiven. The audience couldn't have cared less. Just looking at her was reward in itself as she and Mr. Stone presented the FiFi to Milton Stern for the Perry Ellis Best Men's Package.

At the conclusion of the awards ceremony, before an audience that included Liz Claiborne, Bill Blass, and socialite Charlotte Ford, the board celebrated my twenty-fifth anniversary as executive director of the foundation. Dr. Fernando Aleu did the honors and, in his usual irrepressible style, presented me with a sterling-silver Tiffany globe, which still sits atop an ebony base in an étagé in my home. A silver plaque on the base is inscribed "To Annette Green with heartfelt gratitude for twenty-five years of impressive accomplishments and personal dedication to the Fragrance Industry." A *big* hug and kiss ended this perfect moment.

Another tribute to my twenty-five years with the foundation took place in London. I was elected by the UK fragrance industry to receive the prestigious Hackforth-Jones Award. The award, presented biannually by the fragrance supplier PPF International (in memory of its highly regarded director, Jimmy Hackforth-Jones), recognizing outstanding contribution to the art and science of perfumery in any field. The judging panel was made up of various officials who represented different industry associations in the UK, together with research and technical advisers who had been founding members of the panel. The award was presented to me by Charles Miller-Smith in London. In my acceptance remarks, I was moved to say, "I am particularly pleased to be the first woman in our industry to be so honored."

At FiFi ceremonies a year later, Parfums Stern would introduce Miss Deneuve's namesake fragrance, which erased her seemingly reluctant attendance in 1985. She made her usual breathtaking appearance in anticipation of being awarded the FiFi for Best Women's Fragrance Introduction of the Year. Happily, her fragrance was a winner. She graciously accepted the award from actress and author Jane Seymour and Marty Bloom. Other celebrity presenters on the stage that evening were Paloma Picasso, Halston, and Diane Von Furstenberg.

In the days before the sixteenth annual awards ceremony, when Elizabeth Taylor's Passion was a nominee, I had several visits from Elizabeth Taylor's staff, led by her major domo, Chen Sam. She was born in Cairo to an Egyptian father and an Italian mother. A take-no-prisoners kind of person, she had full authority as Elizabeth's confidante and custodian. She was intent on scoping out emergency exits, just in case. The banquet manager, accustomed to celebrity insecurities, gave us a tour of the innards of the Waldorf Astoria and possible emergency escape routes. Fortunately, none were necessary.

The night of the ceremonies, a special raised platform was set up in a room adjourning the ballroom for a photography and media session with all the celebrity presenters. Everyone was accounted for except Elizabeth Taylor, who was notorious for being tardy. When she and her entourage finally arrived (about an hour late), Chen Sam made it clear to me that Miss Taylor would not move into the room unless I took her by the hand and guided her through the mobs of photographers and attendees.

I was, to say the least, startled by her instruction. I turned to Chen to clarify what she had told me: "You want me to pull Miss Taylor across the room?" That was what she meant, and that is what I did. I have to say, I found myself holding a very small, soft, pliable hand.

Once we arrived at the staging area, she didn't let go, either. As you can imagine, it was unnerving to find myself being photographed with one of the world's most beautiful women. Though she was her usual charming and encouraging self, I departed as fast as possible.

When Elizabeth Taylor attended the FiFi ceremonies in 1992 in anticipation of a second award for White Diamonds, I invited her to be a presenter earlier in the ceremony with man-on-the-moon astronaut Buzz Aldrin. He made quite an impact on the audience in his white officer's jacket, ablaze with medals. She was thrilled and totally in awe of our space hero. Obviously, even great celebrities can be as starstruck as the rest of us.

A Nostalgic Celebration

The industry reminisced about the fortieth anniversary of the Fragrance Foundation at the seventeenth annual awards ceremonies. The ballroom was bathed in a ruby-red glow, and a glittering burst of colorful pulsating lights filled the stage. Golden ribbons spelled out "Memories, 1949–1989." A record number of guests from around the world gathered at the Waldorf Astoria in New York to celebrate and honor the finalists and winners of 1998. We invited celebrities, who each had made their own mark in 1949, to present the FiFis. Movie legend Joan Bennett; supermodel Carmen; stage star Carol Channing; actresses Arlene Dahl, Claire Trevor, and Gloria DeHaven; and the renowned tenor Allan Jones. It was a most nostalgic gathering, and there were many poignant moments.

During the press conference, though, Allan Jones, who had known great fame in the forties and was the father of the popular tenor Jack Jones, had a traumatic encounter with the press. Most were not at all aware of who he was and basically ignored him. I tried to focus their attention, but it didn't happen. Frustrated, Mr. Jones lashed out at the reporters and photographers, accusing them of being ignorant of the stars of the past. His remarks created quite a stir and more than a little embarrassment.

Later that evening, on a lighter note, the entire board of directors lined up on stage for a special salute honoring me for not only saving the Fragrance Foundation back in 1961 but for developing programs that had placed it in the forefront of the industry's growth. I walked down the line, embracing each board member. What an emotional moment. Dr. Fernando Aleu, representing the board, invited me to join him at the mic and presented me with a sterling silver Tiffany tray engraved with the signatures of each board member. I was especially thrilled to learn, too, that the board had voted to establish a perpetual scholarship in my name to benefit students in the new cosmetics marketing curriculum that I had helped establish at the Fashion Institute of Technology.

Carol Channing was one of the FiFi presenters that night, and she surprised me with a gift of a "diamond ring" in honor of the occasion. I still have it as a delightful memento of the star who made *Diamonds Are a Girl's Best Friend* famous and the rest of us very happy.

Unscripted!

As the ceremonies grew in stature, so did competition. In fact, it took twenty-two years before the FiFis inspired other industry organizations to jump into the world of awards. The Cosmetic Executive Women (CEW) was the first. In 1994, the organization announced it would present annual beauty awards to recognize winning products in every category except fragrance (in consideration of the FiFis). Nevertheless, after a few more years, fragrance awards were unceremoniously incorporated into their ceremonies. The board of directors of the Fragrance Foundation was perturbed about the decision and invited the president of CEW, Carlotta Jacobson, and the board's chairwoman, Jean Hoehn Zimmerman, who at that time was executive vice president at Chanel, to meet to discuss a possible conflict.

The meeting did not go well. They disputed any perception of a problem and were determined to proceed with their fragrance awards balloting. Thinking back on the position they took, they were right. Their awards were not competitive. The importance of the FiFis was set in stone as the ultimate award within the fragrance industry here and abroad. It was a good thing, too, because as time went by, other organizations joined the fray. The Fashion Group established beauty and fragrance awards, and so did *Women's Wear Daily*. In retrospect, we learned the more awards, the merrier. They all created a smooth path to the FiFis, just as the Golden

Globes and ever newer movie award ceremonies help to set the motion picture industry and the public afire in anticipation of the Oscars.

Since nothing succeeds like success, the FiFi ceremonies were awash with ever more glorious and glamorous presenters, including models Christie Brinkley and Naomi Campbell, who wore a skintight, see-through black-lace gown. It caused quite a stir, especially when her co-presenter, Donald Trump, with eyes wide open, followed her dangerously close as they climbed the stairs to the stage. TV, movie, and stage stars Rita Moreno, Diahann Carroll, and Isabella Rossellini dazzled the crowd with their very special brand of joie de vivre.

Of course, there were surprises. I was certainly anxious the year the stage and nightclub star, Elaine Stritch, came to the mic to present a couple of FiFi awards and announced she had no idea why she was there. I abandoned the microphone and hurried backstage to where the fabulous six-foot-five dancer, stage star, and raconteur, Tommy Tune, garbed in tie and tails, was waiting for his cue. I urged him to join Elaine—*fast*. He is such a pro (and friend), that he did, and soon they were bantering about the awards without a sign of stress. Nobody ever mentioned what had happened.

Broadway star Tommy Tune with the legendary Elaine Stritch.

In 1994, when we celebrated our twenty-second awards ceremony, there were 1,700 members of the industry in the audience. Among our stars were Christopher Reeve, Julie Wilson, and Karl Lagerfeld. I crossed my fingers when Karl advised me that he was unwilling to stand backstage and would return exactly two minutes before he was introduced. I gave him the time frame, but I certainly had no idea when I introduced him if he would appear or not. But, voilà! There he was.

There was a special tribute that evening that saluted the four saviors of the Fragrance Foundation thirty-three years before. The board of directors established a Fragrance Foundation Founders Scholarship in the names of Paul Martineau, Sydney Friend, Joseph Danilek, and my indispensable and beloved friend and mentor, Jack Mohr, who was seated in a special box overlooking the stage with his family. We blew kisses to each other. The scholarship was to support the students in the cosmetic/fragrance curriculum at the Fashion Institute of Technology, as well as the newly-established Annette Green/Fragrance Foundation Studio.

In 2000, the board enthusiastically concurred with my proposal to create Circle of Champions awards. They were to be presented every November at ceremonies separate and apart from the FiFis. The purpose was to celebrate an individual who had made a notable and newsworthy impact on the fragrance industry within the past ten months.

Recipients were selected by Fragrance Foundation members who were first sent nomination forms. The top three industry visionaries receiving the majority of the nominations were placed on a ballot and sent back to members for a final vote. The results were received and tabulated by the independent accounting firm Grant Thornton LLP.

Leonard Lauder was the first to be elected to the Circle of Champions and was presented the award by TV raconteur and newsman Charlie Rose at ceremonies in the Sky Club atop the Pan Am building. It was an exquisite, perfectly round Steuben crystal, *Concentricity*, created by sculptor Eric Hilton.

The industry voted to honor me two years later. Quite a thrill.

On June 5, 2001, the twenty-ninth FiFi Awards ceremony was held at Radio City Music Hall and for the first time was open to the public. Several hundred tickets were sold through Ticketron, and we expected over a thousand attendees from the international fragrance industry. We were still faced, however, with what seemed like an insurmountable challenge to

fill the cavernous hall of over four thousand seats. In an all-out push, we contacted all of our relatives, friends, and friends of friends we could find to help us "paper the house." We also made a special industry price for blocks of tickets to be sold to companies in the industry to distribute to junior staff members, as well as to salesgirls. When our search was over, we were thrilled to have our audience of about three thousand of our nearest and dearest.

The late Gregory Hines, a much-admired brilliant dancer and raconteur, was my co-host. What fun it was rehearsing with him the day before the ceremony. He spent several hours in my office and took me through my paces in the most playful and relaxing way. The next night, he dazzled the crowd by making his entrance down the invisible stairs, which are part of the glorious hall's art deco wall leading to the stage. Two spectacular performances by the world-famous Radio City Rockettes delighted the audience, and it was fascinating to watch them go through their strenuous rehearsals. And they were so kind to me.

Working on the gigantic Radio City Music Hall stage was more daunting than I had anticipated. At showtime, I was to enter through curtains at the back of the stage and walk under a canopy of canes held up by the Rockettes. The advice they gave me just before I stepped out was to take a really deep breath and *go*. I did and was so focused on my breathing that I lost any feelings of insecurity that I might have had. I crossed what

Gregory Hines, the Rockettes and yours truly.

seemed to me to be an endless expanse leading to the apron of the stage where Gregory was waiting. Though we had a teleprompter, working with Gregory was so relaxing, we really didn't need it. He quipped his way through the ceremonies, and I played his straight sidekick. Part of the fun was the hilarious appearance during the ceremonies of Joan Rivers. She regaled the audience with her very special brand of humor directed at several of the nominees as she presented the awards.

With the overwhelming success of the FiFi Awards in the United States, attended each year by an increasing number of industry members from abroad, the board established focus groups (1989–1990) led by Edie Weiner to evaluate whether or not to take the awards and the foundation international. The answer was obvious. The natural first stop was, of course, Paris. I left on my mission in the spring of 1990 full of enthusiasm for sharing the FiFis with the French. My first meeting was with Robert Le Duc, who at the time was the president of the Federation des Industries de la Parfumerie. My proposal, however, was met with a great deal of skepticism. The French, for one thing, were unsure how well American awards would translate to its constituency. For another, they were not very enthusiastic about the idea being the brainchild of an American woman. With perseverance, however, and the incredible support of Michele Meyer (who was affiliated with Quest), Marie Chantal Fournier (then with International Flavors & Fragrances), and Theo Spilka (of Firmenich), we overcame the doubts and began to make strides. It was touch and go, though, for almost a year.

Merci!

When we finally got the green light, the first ceremonies were held in the Cosmetic Department of the famous department store Galleries Lafayette. Only about forty industry members attended. Obviously, we were just at the beginning of a long journey. Happily, over the years the ceremonies grew dramatically and took on a panache and personality of their own. A major turning point was the influential and indispensable support and guidance of all our efforts by Alain Grange Cabane, who succeeded M. Le Duc as president of the Federation.

Of course, it was still far from smooth sailing for the FiFis, but the awards weathered the turbulence thanks to the dedicated French Fragrance Foundation board members, which included the original supporters I just mentioned, as well as the board's retired president, Catherine Disdet, who at the time was with the fragrance supplier Dragoco. A particularly memorable reception took place in Paris following the awards in a salon overlooking exquisite gardens at the Pavillon D'Armenville. As I relished the view, I realized that the awards had *arrived* in every sense of the word. By 1992, when the French FiFis were awarded, nearly 550 new women's scents and over 250 men's had been launched internationally.

Once the FiFis were a fait accompli in Paris, we went on to introduce them in the UK, Italy, Spain, and Germany. After a series of meetings in each country, we were given the green light. I travelled to all the awards ceremonies every year with my indispensable executive director, Mary Ellen Lapsansky.

Each country's approach was unique.

Thank You!

In London, the industry originally paid tribute to its fragrance honorees at elegant luncheons usually held at the Savoy Hotel in conjunction with the retailing association COPRA. After a couple of years, they transitioned to elegant black-tie affairs.

In the spring of 1994, though, I was asked to speak at one of the luncheons and decided I would focus my remarks on the growing importance of technology and how it would affect the industry:

A funny thing is happening on the way to the information superhighway that is sending messages of olfactory surprises that few of us could have anticipated. Fragrance is fast becoming one of the purchases of choice of the TV travelers on this highway—many of whom are often none the wiser about the scent itself.

There appear to be three big reasons propelling this powerful new marketplace: convenience, service, and choice. They seem obvious, but I found some even more basic concerns fueling the fire.

Fear of crime ... Only 25 percent of American consumers believe that shopping malls provide a safe and secure shopping environment, a major consideration as population grows.

In addition, boredom with shopping is far more pervasive than many of us dare admit: stores that look the same, selling the same merchandise to customers confused by the overwhelming variety, and the fact that consumers have made it crystal clear that they want shopping to be an entertaining, as well as gratifying experience, seems to have eluded some of our most prestigious and powerful marketers and retailers.

No wonder that many of us turn on the TV, and before we've turned it off have purchased a whole range of necessities and luxuries, including products to enhance, products for body and soul. Certainly, at the top of the list of soul soothers is scent.

By the reaction of the audience at the end of my comments, I realized I had shocked everyone, and almost without exception, they rejected my message. A year or so later in an article reassessing what had taken place at the luncheon, an editor of the British trade publication *SPC* reported, "Today they accepted she was absolutely right."

In 2003, I was advised by two board members of the Fragrance Foundation UK, John Ayres and Murray Pierce, of my election as honorary president of the Fragrance Foundation UK. I have no idea if I still am, because after many changes on the board and management of the British satellite, I have never heard another word.

Grazie!

Italy included the FiFi in black-tie awards ceremonies under the auspices of the Accademia del Profumo, which were held annually at an extraordinary estate in the countryside of Bologna. At one of these dinners, the great Luciano Pavarotti was present to accept the award for his new fragrance. His appearance created quite a stir. I have to say he took all the adulation with astonishing grace, despite being forced to forego his dinner by the constant stream of admirers surrounding him.

Many of the industry's leaders lent their presence to the festivities: the influential and charismatic Roberto Martone, president and CEO of ICR and vice president of the distribution arm ITF; inspiring trailblazers Laura Zaccagnini and Florio Terenzi of SoGeCos[3]; and Rosetta and Luciana Parisini, the charming publishers of the influential Italian trade magazine *Allure*.[4] The Parisinis became dear friends and supporters of all our efforts in Italy, for which I am eternally grateful.

In 2003, at its eighth annual FiFi Awards, the Fragrance Foundation Italy presented me with a special Premio Caterina de Medici Award: a 5.5" x 7.5" velvet-backed block frame of sterling silver surrounded a beautiful eighteenth-century drawing of couples enjoying a lovely flower garden. Engraved below it, copy (loosely translated) paid tribute to my "love and passion in service of the world of perfume." It has given me great pleasure and pride to polish it these many years.

Gracias!

In Spain, several of the ceremonies were held in theaters, including the IMEX. Festive cocktail reception/buffets followed in the theater lobbies. And speaking of receptions, each year when Mary Ellen and I arrived in Madrid, we were always accorded the most enthusiastic and generous welcomes. The gentlemen responsible for organizing FiFi in Spain—Enrique Puig, Alex Ventos, Jaime Pla, and Antonio Bergillos—escorted us everywhere. What a charming group of hosts they were as they shared fascinating information about Spain and the industry. We visited key parfumeries and a unique perfume museum located in the back of a parfumerie. To express their appreciation for our presence, they presented us with memorable gifts of beautiful porcelains by Lladró—a charming seated little girl embracing a delicate bouquet of flowers one year and a dramatic flamenco dancer the next. During one of my visits, Spanish *Vogue* invited me to sit for a pen-and-ink drawing. The illustrator's impressionistic view appeared in an upcoming edition of the magazine. The editor kindly gave me the original drawing. It hangs on my bedroom wall at home these days.

For a variety of internal reasons, Spain eventually announced it was not able to continue the award ceremonies. It was a decision we all regretted.

Danke!

Germany's FiFi ceremonies were black-tie dinner affairs, under the brilliant direction of Heinz-Walter Hinrichs. One of the most memorable ceremonies took place at the Kempinski Atlantic Hotel in Hamburg. Karl Lagerfeld was also an honoree that night. In 2000, a prestigious jury of members of the Frankfurt Fair and the German Federation of Perfumery Retailers chose me to receive the second annual Beauty World Cup 2000 Award. The award was conceived to honor particular achievements in perfumery and cosmetics. It was presented before an audience of approximately six hundred members of the international fragrance industry by Reinhard-Dieter Wolf for "a life's work and tireless dedication to the fragrance industry." In my acceptance remarks, I expressed deep appreciation and "a very special joy to be honored for having an endless love affair with one's life work." Participating in the ceremonies were Michael von Zitzewitz, chairman of the board management at Frankfurt Fair, and Peter Alois, commercial consul, American consulate, Frankfurt, Germany.

Three years later, in recognition of my retirement, the German Fragrance Foundation presented me with the prestigious FiFi Ehren Award (Karl Lagerfeld had received the same honor a few years earlier). It recognizes "an individual who has made a significant contribution to promoting fragrance as a cultural asset and as an important economic factor and has worked to prevent the increasing trivialization of fragrance." A slender, twelve-inch-round, sterling silver obelisk topped by a silver ball and set on a circular dark-brown wooden base, the award is a constant reminder of the extraordinary fragrance industry and its leaders in Germany.

Each country reached out to local celebrities from the TV and movie worlds to emcee their ceremonies. I was always asked to co-present the awards. This was particularly daunting during the mid-nineties when I had broken my foot in an accident at a CTFA convention in Florida. It had to be encased in a protective boot for more than four months. The timing couldn't have been worse, since it coincided with the European awards schedule. Nevertheless, I was determined to attend all of the ceremonies, though supported by a cane and with the help of Mary Ellen. I have to say it was a challenge but gave me heroic status in the eyes of the FiFi organizers and gala attendees in each country, who did everything possible to accommodate my limited mobility.

Farewell to All That

I produced my last US FiFi ceremony in 2002. We were back in Avery Fisher Hall at Lincoln Center. Davie Lerner designed a joyful, color-drenched set to accommodate our first live onstage orchestra. We were celebrating the thirtieth anniversary of the awards, and I wanted it to be memorable in every way. I had the good fortune to be introduced to the jazz master Jay Leonhart,[5] who agreed to put together a group of his favorite musicians, including a vocalist, who would perform for the ceremonies. They were tremendous and in full swing as the surprised and enthusiastic audience entered the hall.

After the last award was presented, my pounding heart gave me pause. The moment had come to announce my retirement. In opening remarks, I took the advice of my friend, actress Arlene Dahl, an expert numerologist, who reminded me that the number thirty (anniversary or no) signifies "the end of the story." I should have remembered that from my newspaper days. I spoke of it and ended my farewell with the promise I would always be the industry's cheerleader. The audience reacted by standing up as one. I moved, as if drawn by an invisible hand, to center stage and bowed. It was a glorious though bittersweet moment.

---

1. Before the onslaught of celebrities, most well-known personalities appeared in industry ads to promote existing fragrances. Norma Gerber, senior editor of *Product Management Magazine*, wrote a perceptive article on the subject in the June 1973 issue, headlined "Do Testimonials Really Work?" She subtitled her article, "Many cosmetic and toiletry firms swear by them but experts claim they are not used effectively." Among the celebrities featured in ad campaigns were Veruschka for Lanvin's My Sin perfume; Deneuve was the famous face for Chanel; and Joe Namath was first the spokesperson for Revlon's Pub Cologne and in later years, the celebrity image for Brut by Faberge.

2. Tavern on the Green in Central Park in New York City was the scene of a festive gala held by Women's Project Theatre in the summer of 1997. The organization, of which I eventually became chairperson of the board, has supported women playwrights for over twenty-five years. At their annual fundraisers, they honor stars of the entertainment world and a member of the business community. Happily, I was invited to join Stockard Channing, Marilyn Horne, and Rosie O'Donnell as an honoree. I chose TV host and raconteur Robin Leach, star of the hit TV show *Lifestyles of the Rich and Famous*, to present my award, which recognized not only my contributions to the fragrance industry over the past thirty-five years but also my commitment to social issues. We all received magnificent engraved crystal spheres. In my acceptance remarks, I shared my lifelong love affair with the theater and admitted I had always considered myself a "Broadway baby." Still do! In fact, the theater in particular and the arts in general have become the focus of my life since retirement.

3. At that time, SoGeCos was in the planning stage of developing an international trade show, Cosmoproof, which today is an important global showcase for the beauty industry.

4. To chronicle the seventh annual ceremony in Italy, *Allure* published an elegant hardcover, four-color book overflowing with memorable photographs of the ceremony.

5. Jay Leonhart is considered one of the finest bassists in the jazz and popular music worlds. A songwriter, poet, and performer, he has played with such greats as Sting, Judy Garland, Frank Sinatra, Tony Bennett, and Marian McPartland.

IV

Confessions of an Exhibitionist

Favorite Co-conspirators

Marc Rosen, vice president of design and communication at Elizabeth Arden

Kitty D'Alessio, vice chairman of Chanel's New Ventures and Special Projects Department, and past president and member of the foundation board

Jerry Lawton, president, Designgroup

Elaine Dee, curator of drawing and prints, Cooper Hewitt

Margo Scavardo, VP, DMM, The Broadway

Toni Hopkins, VP/DMM at Neiman Marcus

Lawrence Aiken, vice president of the foundation board and president, Parfums Givenchy

Lawrence Pesin, secretary of the foundation board and president, Colonia

Richard Martin, professor of history of civilization and art, dean of the division of graduate study, and director of the museum at FIT

Philip Shearer, president, Perfume and Beauty Division, Cosmair, and foundation board chairman

In order to create, there must be a dynamic force. And what force is more potent than love?

—Igor Stravinsky

In the early seventies, as we focused the foundation on expanding the public's appreciation of the world of sweet smells, my infatuation with the idea of fragrance as an art form took a major turn. I convinced the board that a relationship with the world of museums and art galleries would go a long way in helping to dramatically spotlight perfume as one of the most personal and appealing artistic achievements. I wasn't sure where to begin but decided to focus on the history of scent from its earliest recorded beginnings.

In the twentieth century, perfumers took a giant leap into modernity. They owed this breakthrough to developments in organic chemistry. New compounds were suddenly available that would change the creation of perfumes forever. First and foremost were the aldehydes, which gave fragrance formulae a "sparkling" lift. Quick to explore its possibilities, the master Chanel perfumer Ernest Beaux conceived a perfume in which he would blend this new and provocative aroma chemical with an array of ingredients found in nature. The result was the legendary Chanel No. 5, which is recognized as the first aldehydic perfume.

It was a historic turning point for the fragrance industry. Perfumers around the globe began to imagine ever more complex and intriguing aromas, no longer only defined by what nature had to offer. The arrival of aroma chemicals also allowed perfumers to meet changing environmental needs by mimicking and replacing animal ingredients, as well as being a stand-in for any flowers, roots, woods, or herbs that might, for one reason or another, be unavailable or unstable.

Housing these olfactory works of art has long been a creative endeavor in its own right. Talented bottle and box designers here and abroad have dedicated themselves to giving an irresistible visible presence to what is essentially invisible. The perfect color combination, accented by the most eye-appealing logos, typefaces, and tactile allures are the necessary ingredients. It's never been an easy pairing, and the wrong visualization can (and did) spell failure for a fragrance. Only the most intuitive, artfully conceived packaging can speak to the unspoken sensory pleasures waiting to be experienced.

Armed with fascinating insights into the past, I began to imagine an exhibition devoted to the historical significance of scents. I prepared a proposal and took a chance and presented it to several staff members of the privately owned Huntington Hartford Museum on Columbus Circle. (now the Museum of Art and Design). The reaction was positive. We discussed the possibility of mounting an exhibition tracing the earliest history of fragrance that I dubbed *Scents of Civilization*. Although the foundation did not have the money to develop a major show, we were assigned an elegant space and the necessary display cases for artifacts, including an ancient civet horn, which I had inherited when I took over the foundation. A well-attended reception by the industry celebrated the opening of the exhibition, which was on view at the museum for over a month and was well received by the public.

My next foray into the art world, in 1981, owed a debt of gratitude to Adriana Zahn, then president of the prestigious National Arts Club on Gramercy Park in New York. I was a member of the club and served on its board. Adriana became quite interested in the creative work of the Fragrance Foundation, which I had shared with her. She felt that it deserved to receive the club's citation of merit for identifying and preserving the little-known subject of fragrance in the arts.

She requested that I develop an exhibition relating fragrance to art, music, architecture, and theater. Fortunately, we had photographs and other memorabilia in the foundation's archives that allowed us to mount a fascinating overview in the galleries of the club.

A gala dinner celebrated the opening, which was attended by the members of the foundation, as well as members of the club. Dr. Fernando Aleu accepted the citation from Mrs. Zahn, which lauded the Fragrance Foundation "for its significant research in identifying the historic relationship of fragrance to the arts. In presenting this citation, the board of governors and the eighty-third anniversary ball committee join us in recognizing and paying tribute to the role that fragrance has played in inspiring artistic expression."

The success of my efforts spurred me on. This time, also in 1981, happenstance was the impetus. I was window shopping along Fifth Avenue. When I reached the Steuben Glass Galleries at Fifth Avenue and 56th Street, I was intrigued by a display of snuff bottles in the windows that reflected a major exhibition inside. As remarkable as those bottles were, as far as I was concerned, they didn't compare to the visual beauty of many historic and contemporary perfume bottles.

When I got back to my office, I called the Public Relations Department of Steuben and suggested the possibility of mounting an exhibition in cooperation with the Fragrance Foundation. There was an immediate interest, prompted by the existence of their own legendary collection of historic perfume bottles in the Corning Glass Museum located at their headquarters in Corning, New York. I was unaware of this museum, but the more I learned, the more astounded I was by the breadth, depth, and historical integrity of the collection.

After about six months of planning and securing appropriate bottles and boxes, as well as posters and related literature, Steuben's creative team from the Corning Glass Museum and the New York gallery at Steuben developed an exquisitely mounted exhibition. I named it *Small Wonders*, and the executives of Steuben reported that it attracted the largest attendance of men and women of any exhibition that had been held in the galleries to that point. I was on a roll and ready to move into the big time.

In 1986, I had the good fortune to hear about an arts group working in tandem with Hoving Associates, a museum consulting firm founded by Thomas Hoving, the legendary retired director of the Metropolitan Museum of Art.

Called Designgroup, its president was a terrific fellow, Jerry Lawton. In fact, in Thomas Hoving's memoir, *Artful Tom*, published in 2000, he said of Jerry, "I have seldom encountered a more intelligent and ethical human being."

Jerry's firm was all about being a conduit to prestigious museums around the world—perfect timing, since I was dreaming about developing an exhibition that would reflect the impact of societal attitudes about scent from the 1800s to the 1900s. After several meetings with Jerry, he proposed we take the concept to the Museum of the City of New York. We met with the then director Robert R. McDonald and his staff. They agreed on the spot to dedicate a full floor to the exhibition, which I proposed we call *Scents of Time—Reflections of Fragrance and Society—1870s to 1900s.*

Once the commitment was made by the museum, I turned to one of the fragrance industry's rising young stars, Marc Rosen. A year or two earlier, he had produced a gorgeous exhibition tracing the history of Elizabeth Arden and her company at the Fashion Institute of Technology. I was convinced he would be the perfect person to work with us on the exhibition.

I invited Marc to lunch at Orsini's, one of New York's "hot" restaurants in the eighties, and I shared the details of what we were planning. Sensing his enthusiasm, I asked if he would like to consider becoming the exhibition chairman. His resounding and immediate *yes* set my plans into high gear. As they developed, Marc worked on every detail of the exhibition, including designing the logo based on an historical flower clock that I had come across in one of our old reference books in the foundation's library.

The museum chose Deborah Samson Shinn to be guest curator. She brought extraordinary expertise and experience to the project and was

Joining Marc Rosen and his actress wife Arlene Dahl.

instrumental in reaching out to private collectors and museums here and abroad for rarely seen materials. Kitty D'Alessio was very influential in helping to gather together historical materials from Chanel, as well as from other members of the industry. One of the major private contributors, author and antique dealer Christie Mayer Lefkowith, contacted me after reading about my plans in the press. As luck would have it, she was an avid collector of historical perfume bottles and generously opened up her home and allowed us to choose from a treasure trove of rare bottles and boxes that were crammed in every nook and cranny. Thanks, too, to a longtime friendship with perfume bottle aficionado and author Ken Leach, who had another rare source for antique perfume bottles, which were housed in his historical perfume-bottle-filled shop at the Manhattan Art & Antique Center. Both Christie and Ken, acclaimed for each having published magnificent coffee-table books on perfume bottles and their lineage, were indispensable to the quality of the memorabilia to be displayed in the exhibition. They also lent their incredible knowledge to preparing the pieces for exhibition.

Because the Museum of the City of New York had a remarkable archive of historical costumes, it was decided to feature mannequins throughout the show, appropriately garbed to reflect the times in which they were worn. Phyllis Magidson, the brilliant curator of costumes and textiles at the museum, created an exciting visual dimension to the show.

Eager to give attendees an olfactory treat that would reflect the types of scents popular in each decade, we enlisted the talents of the industry's top perfumers to develop the scents based on our historical information. Leaflets featuring fragrance burst scent samplers provided by 3M were placed throughout the exhibition in Lucite wall holders. Each of the samplers included two unique fragrances, along with a history of the scents and a description of the era in which they were developed. Included were the eau de cologne from the perfumed court of Louis XV, the essence of rose worn by Empress Josephine, along with such twentieth-century fragrances as an exhilarating spice that first became popular in the forties. The leaflets were available for attendees to take, which allowed them to enjoy these long-forgotten smell impressions.

In honor of the historic exhibition, the perfumers of Roure Bertrand Dupont created Scents of Time, a fragrance to express contemporary sensory attitudes. The fragrance, a fresh floral bouquet with a crisp green top note, was specially formulated for the fragrance fountain in the beautiful marble lobby of the Museum of the City of New York, as well as in other host museums. Pierre Dinand, the spectacular French perfume bottle designer who created the splendid FiFi crystal sculpture, contributed a reproduction of historic seventeenth-century "picture frame" perfume bottles, thanks to a mold he found in a Paris flea market. The glass bottle featured a blank two-by-two-inch square indented in the glass at its center, surrounded by a raised floral design, into which a photograph, drawing, or a Scents of Time label could be affixed. The bottle became a favorite in the gift shops of the museums exhibiting *Scents of Time*, as did books on perfume and its glamorous packaging. We also gave the bottle to guests attending each exhibition gala. To add to the festive environment, Parfums Givenchy generously contributed Veuve Clicquot champagne.

All the hard work in gathering the hundreds of objects and all the related materials—and developing the environment in which they would be displayed—finally came to fruition in the fall of 1987. The curtain went up at a much anticipated opening-night party for the industry and members of the museum. Hosted by the foundation, klieg lights lit up the sky on Fifth Avenue and fancifully costumed mimes whimsically extended greetings as the attendees stepped back in time to enter the exhibition through a giant replica of the *Scents of Time* logo. Inside the gallery, over two hundred *objets d'art*, including bottles, boxes, figurines, porcelains, advertisements, posters, labels, books, fans, and fashions were presented in a sparkling space designed by Jeffrey Strean. A fascinating video was produced by Gorman Communications to showcase the mores of society over the decades. We created a special theater-like installation for viewing the video. It was a great hit, and after the exhibition closed, the video was in demand in and out of the industry.

The exhibition had a run from October 6, 1987, to February 7, 1988, and received terrific press reviews, including in the *New York Times*. It was a major success, with a record number of attendees. As an added attraction, we held special Sunday events for grown-ups, as well as for children.

I have to admit I was absolutely besotted with *Scents of Time*. I couldn't keep away from the museum and visited several times a week. I loved listening to viewers' opinions (happily, very good) and checking the housekeeping and condition of the materials available to the public (always perfect). I became the resident panel moderator every weekend for the discussions we arranged with a wide range of experts, including collectors Christie Lefkowith and Ken Leach, as well as Elaine Dee, Paul Hollister (glass expert and author of *A Stroll through a Glass Garden*), and George Ratafia (international art dealer and antique fragrance label collector). For the exhibition, he lent us historic perfume bottle labels in handpainted, gold-leaf frames. Rare and extraordinary, they caused quite a sensation.

When the exhibition closed, there was no question that I did suffer withdrawal symptoms. Fortunately, I became so involved with getting the show on the road to the next four museum destinations that I did not have too much time to brood about the New York closing.

In conjunction with Designgroup, arrangements were made for the exhibition to travel cross-country. The first stop was the newly opened National Museum of Women in the Arts in Washington, D.C., and was followed by exhibitions at the Museum of Science and Industry in Chicago and the California Museum of Science and Industry in Los Angeles. The exhibition ended its run on April 30, 1989, at the Science Place in Dallas, Texas.

Excitement surrounding the arrival of *Scents of Time* was palpable. Jerry Lawton and his team were constants at my side in each city as we joined museum VIPs, curators, gala chairs, socialites, local newsmakers, and retailers to celebrate the openings at black-tie soirees. Contingents from the Fragrance Foundation in New York and regional fragrance company members, including the chair of the exhibition, Marc Rosen, were also on hand to open the ceremonies at all the venues. Local media was lavish in its praise from New York to Dallas.

Perfume on the Potomac

In Washington, guests from the diplomatic, government, and social worlds gathered, danced, and dined under the museum's glittering crystal chandeliers in the grand rotunda. I joined the museum's founder and president of the board, Mrs. Wilhelmina Cole Holladay, and Mrs. Daniel Joseph Callahan III, chairperson of the black-tie gala, in a reception line to welcome the elegant attendees.[1] Everyone received fragrance gifts courtesy of foundation members.

Retailers saluted the arrival of Scents of Time with a marvelous variety of Fragrance Week events for shoppers to enjoy. Garfinckel's dedicated three major windows to eighteen-inch first lady dolls (borrowed from the Smithsonian) of Martha Washington, Dolley Madison, Edith Roosevelt, Grace Coolidge, and Mamie Eisenhower and displayed the favorite fragrances of their eras as documented by White House historians. The Hecht Company took advantage of its Thirteenth Street windows, which faced the museum, by silk-screening the *Scents of Time* logo and directions to the museum on the glass windows. Other retailers heralded the exhibition with window and in-store displays and fragrance sampling. The exhibition video and posters, a specially designed *Glamour* magazine, calendars, and the commemorative picture-frame perfume bottles were all integrated into in-store celebrations.

Chicago Bound

An international group of fragrance industry leaders from Paris and New York celebrated the festivities at the opening of the *Scents of Time* exhibition at the Chicago Museum of Science and Industry. They were entertained in the flower-filled gallery by strolling violinists Franz Benteler and the Royal

Strings. Commissioner of Cultural Affairs Joan Harris, representing the office of the acting mayor of Chicago, and Dr. Jerry Khan, president of the museum, were among the honored guests. The commissioner presented the mayor's proclamation saluting the first Fragrance Week in Chicago to Kitty D'Alessio, president of the foundation's board of directors.

The Chicago Museum expanded the exhibition by adding a fascinating three-part scientific module featuring ingredient sources from around the world, the art and science of fragrance creation, and the science of the sense of smell. The module was developed by a group of fragrance supplier members of the foundation.[2]

Vice President John Stabenau of Marshall Field's Cosmetics Department chaired the retail committee with local perfume marketers[3] to support *Scents of Time* in a citywide celebration. Colorful banners flew from streetlamps in front of the flagship stores of Carson Pirie Scott and Marshall Field's. During Fragrance Week, horse-drawn carriages, sponsored by a different manufacturer every day, were gaily decorated with announcements of the exhibition. They traveled up and down Michigan Avenue and State Street, with models dressed in fashions evoking the different eras featured in *Scents of Time*, distributing fragrance samples to the public. Twenty-five thousand visited the exhibition during its three-month run.

Los Angeles Love-In

Colorfully-costumed heralds welcomed guests with a trumpeted fanfare as they arrived at the steps leading to the entry of the California Museum of Science and Industry in Los Angeles. Banners, imprinted with the *Scents of Time* insignia, decorated each golden trumpet. The glorious rose garden on the grounds of the museum created a perfect sensory environment as glamorous models, musicians, and dancers led a procession that began on the terrace overlooking the garden and the pool fountain to the reception. Celebrities Rosemary and Robert Stack co-chaired the gala committee, which included Jane Seymour, Mrs. Henry Mancini, Louis Estevez, and Arlene Dahl. An elegant press breakfast in Los Angeles was underwritten by Bijan Fragrances and hosted by Mr. Bijan.

All major California retailers hosted tables at an elegant dinner that evening.[4] The worlds of fashion and fragrance joined to entertain diners with elegant tableaux (shades of my 1975 costume promenade, chapter II), featuring vivacious models dressed in lavish historical costumes and luxurious designer evening gowns. Nineteen of the world's great fragrances were worn by the models courtesy of famous fragrance houses.[5] A retail committee, which coordinated Fragrance Week events in the city, was chaired by Margo Scavarda working hand in hand with JoAnn Marshall, divisional vice president of the May Company. Roses Inc., courtesy of the Rose Growers of California, contributed five thousand roses for the guests, with a thousand being divided between ten participating retailers to distribute to customers at the opening.

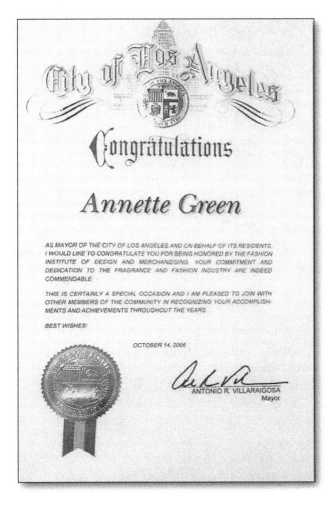

Texas Show-Closer

Legendary Texas hospitality was a force to be reckoned with at the Science Place when *Scents of Time* arrived in Dallas. The exhibition was handsomely mounted in a three-thousand-square-foot sunlit gallery. A pre-Valentine gala, held in the great hall of the museum, celebrated the opening. Guests were invited to wear the color evoked by their favorite fragrance. Everyone was greeted by flower-bedecked dinosaurs and toasted the exhibition's triumphant arrival at the last venue on its cross-country tour. Festivities included cocktails, a buffet, and dancing. *Ultra* magazine was the underwriter of the evening, which benefited the museum, as did an auction that included lavish fragrance gifts donated by foundation members. *HG* magazine and Nina Ricci provided the flowers, and Neiman Marcus offered gift bags of fragrances for all attendees. Everyone also received the *Scents of Time* commemorative journal.

The Honorable Annette Strauss, mayor of Dallas, and Richard F. Coyne, president and chief executive officer of the Science Place, joined together for the ribbon-cutting ceremony. Retail support was led by Chairperson Toni Hopkins and her committee of leading Dallas retailers.[6] Lawrence Aiken and Lawrence Pesin flew in from New York to join the festivities, as did Hannon Bunning, vice president of Firmenich, and Manfred Pawlak, one of the company's top perfumers. Co-chairs of the gala, socialite Carole Ann Brown and Norma Myers, chairman and editor in chief of *Ultra*, joined me in leading guests through the exhibition.

New York Reentry

Soon after the exhibition finished its final run in Dallas, the Fragrance Foundation was invited to participate in an exhibition to take place in the museum at the Fashion Institute of Technology in New York to be called *Jocks & Nerds*. It was to be devoted to the multifaceted roles played by American men in the twentieth century and the image-creating power of fashion and fragrance. The exhibition was curated by Richard Martin and Harold Koda.

I turned again to Marc Rosen to work with Richard and Harold to design the imaginative and fun-filled décor. Miniature lights glittered on branches of ficus trees, walls were bathed in a soft-pink glow, and a group of life-size cut-out figures of John Wayne, Fred Astaire, Jerry Lewis, Jimmy Stewart, and Henry Fonda surprised guests at the preview party. Business executives from the fashion and fragrance worlds mingled with models dressed in costumes that related to the twelve types of men featured in the exhibition: cowboy, jock, joe college, businessman, man about town, rebel, military man, worker, nerd, hunter, sportsman, and dandy.

Elizabeth Arden, Benetton Cosmetics, Colonia, and Prince Matchabelli hosted the party, and Parfums Givenchy added to the festivities with Veuve Clicquot champagne. Giant factices of fragrance bottles provided by members of the Fragrance Foundation were prominently exhibited in a huge display case resembling a man's medicine chest. Also on display were some of the most provocative men's fragrance advertisements created over the years. Attendees at the opening night party were treated to gift bags provided by A&S, Benetton, Bergdorf Goodman, Cartier, Lord & Taylor, and Saks Fifth Avenue, filled with men's fragrance samples and copies of our brochure, *The Male Fragrance Adventure*. Guests also received fragrance bursts, generously provided by 3M, featuring olfactory impressions created by perfumers from Haarmann & Reimer, Felton Worldwide, and Roure to reveal the masculine fragrance personalities that dominated the ten decades.

TV Commercials Remembered

I worked with the Fashion Institute of Technology once more in the mid-nineties on an exhibition that I had proposed celebrating TV fragrance commercials. Package designer Georges Gotlib created a memorable logo interpreting *Seeing Scents*, my title for the show. It turned out to be an excellent educational vehicle for the students at FIT who were enrolled in the cosmetic/fragrance marketing program. It also attracted members of the advertising and marketing community and the fragrance industry, who were fascinated by the first-time viewing of the earliest perfume commercials. They were shown on a giant TV set located in the lobby of the Shirley Goodman Resource Center on the FIT campus.

It would not be until the end of the twentieth century that I would have the thrill of developing and creating America's first fragrance museum to be housed in a newly acquired space at the Fragrance Foundation. The chairman of the board, Philip Shearer, surprised me with the announcement on stage at the beginning of the 1999 FiFi ceremony that the board had voted unanimously to name the new museum for me. In making the announcement, he said, "Annette has long been the workhorse of the Fragrance Foundation. Tonight, she is our muse." I was absolutely speechless and thrilled, and I was only able to carry on with the awards ceremony by sheer force of will.

The Annette Green Museum at the Fragrance Foundation opened to the public on Monday, November 8, 1999. In coverage on the Friday before, *Women's Wear Daily* reported, "The fragrance industry will reach a milestone with the opening of the first museum in the United States devoted to the history of scent."

A preopening party was held in the fifteen-hundred-square-foot gallery. It was attended by over five hundred members of the industry and media. Philip Shearer greeted the attendees and expressed his belief that "the museum will promote the fragrance industry in the public's eye, tangibly connecting several decades of fragrance."

Proud to welcome Evelyn Lauder, Senior Corporate Vice President of Estée Lauder.

The museum immediately enjoyed strong support from the beauty industry. At the reception, the museum was presented a $50,000 check by Condé Nast, which published a twenty-page outset touting the museum in its December issues of *Vogue, Glamour, Mademoiselle, Vanity Fair*, and *Allure*. The outset also served as the exhibition's program.

Jasmine.com and Creed co-sponsored an exhibition and sale of perfume bottles (from the collection of Christie Meyer Lefkowith) to benefit the museum. The sale was held online at the Jasmin.com website and at a reception. It resulted in the purchase of thirty-four vintage fragrance bottles valued in excess of $25,000. The bottles were donated to the museum and added to its permanent collection. According to Dale Dewey, president and CEO of the website, the bottles were contributions from Christie Lefkowitz's collection. She also was curator of his online museum and author of the gorgeous coffee-table book *The Art of Perfume*. Ms. Lefkowith served as vice president of the board of the Annette Green Museum.

Thanks to the largesse of five of the industry's leading fragrance suppliers (whose presidents were members of the board of the Fragrance Foundation), the museum was the beneficiary of important additions to its collection. Geoffrey Webster of Givaudan Roure contributed a series of

"Spirit of Perfume" sculpture by Erte.

Happy moments with Senior Account Manager Wes Morris and
General Manager of Quest International Herb Kelhoffer.

fragrance-themed watercolors and a voluptuous bronze sculpture by the
art deco artist Erté called *Spirit of Perfume*. Though most of Erté's famous
sculptures feature standing, glamorously clad women, this one revealed a
reclining nude holding a bottle of perfume above her head as she gazed
at it rapturously. Two rare French fragrance-themed vintage posters were
donated by Firmenich's Paterick Firmenich. Dragoco's Dan Stebbins also
arranged for the museum to receive two historic posters.

A fifty-year timeline tracing the history of the Fragrance Foundation was
commissioned by Eugene Grisanti of International Flavors & Fragrances.
The timeline was mounted on the wall of the museum's new conference
center, which housed the foundation's extensive library. A souvenir mini
version of the timeline, which was distributed to members of the industry,
museum visitors, and media, was funded by Quest International thanks to
its president, Demi Thoman.

Other gifts to the museum included two elegant eighteenth-century
Adams cabinets from Elizabeth Arden, courtesy of its president and
foundation board member, Peter England. There were also loans of
vintage and contemporary perfume bottles and memorabilia from many
other fragrance industry members, which added real heft to the museum's

holdings. All the exhibitions were designed by Robin Parkinson and Zette Emmons. I served as curator.

The first exhibition was dedicated to the theme "50 Years of Fragrance in America." It featured a time capsule of 250 scents popular from the fifties through the nineties. A video highlighted fragrance commercials from 1949 to the present. A special area was created to house a "smelling scenter," in which visitors could find and smell popular single fragrance notes of the past fifty years, including chocolate, vanilla, and musk.

In May 2000, the museum presented its second exhibition, *FAB FiFi Nights: The Stars! The FiFi Awards! The Winning Scent-sations!* The exhibition was a glamorous, glitzy, Hollywood-style tribute. Winners over the past twenty-seven years starred in the exhibition, as did the history, celebrities, and glamour of the award ceremonies.

The third exhibition examined the extraordinary and fanciful history of men and their fragrances from the seventeenth century to the twenty-first. The exhibit was the first to record the historical journey of male fragrance usage and the societal impact of men's fragrance dating back to the seventeenth century and the Napoleonic era. More than three hundred objects were featured in the exhibition, including rare historic pieces highlighted by an array of men's hats that had never been seen before in the public domain.

Sex, Scents and Cinema was the fourth exhibition, focusing on the use of fragrance in movies to attract the opposite sex. The generous, savvy, and irrepressible movie critic, actor, author, and Hollywood aficionado Rex Reed, who I met through my friends Marc Rosen and Arlene Dahl, offered to dig into his archives. As luck would have it, he found and loaned us rare old movie clips and stills in which perfume played fascinating supporting roles to some very famous actresses, including Marilyn Monroe. Who can forget the glamour girl's naughty response, "Chanel No. 5," to the question, "What do you wear to bed?" Made headlines!

Rex helped edit and narrate the historic tape, which frankly became the hit of the exhibition. On opening night, he acted as our master of ceremonies and regaled the crowd with insider stories revealing Hollywood's early take on the role of perfume and sexual allure. He credited the famous director Cecil B. DeMille for being amongst the first, early in the twentieth century, to make the link. The film was the long forgotten *Why Change Your Wife?* According to Rex, however, it was George Cukor who gave perfume and its power to seduce really meaningful on-screen billing in the classic film *The Women*. Fans, then and now, aren't likely to forget the sexual machinations of Joan Crawford in her role as a glamorous, predatory perfume saleslady.

Rex also pointed out that perfume often became a prop, replacing dialogue when the script called for emotional revelations. "If a character was pictured angrily throwing a perfume bottle against a wall," he explained, "it was understood she was emotionally distraught—probably by a love lost. Furthermore, if an actress was subtle in her application of perfume (just a touch behind the earlobes and the base of the throat), she was recognized by the audience for her ladylike qualities." The opposite, it seems, was true if the character appeared to be heavy-handed perfume user. She was marked as a 'fallen' woman." I might add, in those straight-laced days, leading ladies who appeared on screen wearing dark lipstick and heavy makeup were faced with the same fate.

After the exhibition closed, the provocative and informative video was sought after for student viewing by educational facilities, including New York's Fashion Institute of Technology and the Fashion Institute for Design and Merchandising in California. Both devote curriculum to fragrance studies.

Lost Opportunity

In early 2000, I was approached by Thomas F. Shutte, president of the renowned Pratt Institute, which had recently established a New York presence on Fourteenth Street. What he had in mind was to offer the Fragrance Foundation the opportunity to relocate the Annette Green Fragrance Museum to a space on the ground floor of his new seven-story building. A high-traffic location, it would not only allow the museum to attract the general public but it would serve as an educational destination for Pratt students attending classes in the building. President Shutte also proposed having his design students develop a spacious environment to accommodate our *objets d'arts*, as well as office and storage space. It was an exciting prospect, since it would move the museum from its out-of-sight current home on the eleventh floor of the Fragrance Foundation offices to an easy walk-in access. President Shutte assured me he was willing to make every possible concession so costs of rent and construction would not be prohibitive. I could hardly wait to give the good news to the board. I didn't realize, however, that because of my impending retirement and the lack of interest on the part of my successor in continuing to spearhead support of the museum (which was not a low-cost endeavor), its future was not at all assured. In fact, in no time at all, I saw the handwriting on the wall and had to turn down President Shutte's offer.

Final Curtain

In the meantime, we developed what would be our last exhibition, *The Lure and Lore of Perfume Classics*, which opened in November 2002. Among the great perfume legends in the exhibition were the fragrances that had been voted into the Fragrance Hall of Fame. To qualify, these classics had to have been fragrance favorites for fifteen years or more. All had a history or a biography that were inseparable from the context in which they were conceived, experienced, and perceived. The exhibition provided biographies of each fragrance throughout its life, including how it was marketed and advertised. In April 2003, the exhibition closed—and so, sadly, did the museum.

It was inconceivable to me that the industry would allow it to slip away. It had attracted so much attention from the American public, students, media, visitors from around the world, and members of the foundation. After just a few years of its existence, the museum had also become an international tourist destination. Having a bona fide perfume museum had placed fragrance outside the boundaries of the commercial world and given it a degree of status and appeal that could not be replicated in any other environment. If ever there was an opportunity for the industry to build on the potential the fragrance museum offered as a unique and timeless marketing magnet, this was it. I searched for allies within the industry, but they were nowhere to be found. In fact, I hadn't realized there were those in very high places who never really had embraced the museum. I couldn't help but wonder, if it had been "a rose by any other name," would the naysayers have turned into enthusiasts. Nevertheless, I was determined not to allow the museum disappear. I set my sights on LA.

Westward Bound

My search resulted in serious discussions with Robert Nelson, the director of the Museum & Galleries at the Fashion Institute for Design & Merchandising (FIDM) in Los Angeles. I had a relationship with the institute for several years as a member of its advisory board. It supported the college's efforts to develop a cosmetic marketing program, under the direction of Irene Cotter, a longtime member of the beauty industry. The program was similar to the one I had helped create at the Fashion Institute of Technology in New York in the seventies. Robert was most enthusiastic about having the perfume museum as a part of his Museum & Galleries, and after meeting with the dynamic top brass at the institute—including its president, Toni Hohberg, Lyn Tobman, department chairperson of the Beauty Industry, Merchandising, and Marketing School, and Barbara Bundy, vice president of education—I felt extremely confident that this transfer would not only save the museum but bring new energy and excitement to its existence.

Once the museum's New York board of trustees agreed to the transfer, I discovered that closing down a museum in New York was not easy. It had not been a piece of cake to get permission to open the museum, either. At the time, the attorney general's office questioned the reasoning behind the museum being named for me. It seems the honor is almost always bestowed upon a generous benefactor. Once they were convinced that the Fragrance Foundation board would fund the museum and had unanimously voted to the naming in tribute to my long dedication and contributions, our lawyers were allowed to move forward. The same attorney general's office that had hesitantly issued the necessary permits to open the new museum in the first place was loath to allow an arts institution to close its doors without clear proof of the necessity. The foundation's lawyers had to prepare in-depth documentation for the New York Supreme Court (county of New York), which in the final analysis issued a dissolution permission. It took months before the deed was done. Not a happy time, I can assure you.

In 2004, the gift of the museum's entire collection, including over a thousand vintage and contemporary bottles and boxes from more than 165 international fragrance houses, perfumers, and private collectors, moved to the Fashion Institute of Design and Merchandising in Los Angeles. The transfer was completed in January 2005. The plans for housing the collection included remodeling an existing space adjacent to the reception area on the second floor of the Los Angeles campus. This space was designed to provide a permanent home for a portion of the collection.

In October 2006, the Annette Green Perfume Museum opened in the FIDM Museum & Galleries with a full-blown exhibition called *Fashion Makes Scents*. Of course, I attended the gala party, as did New York members of the fragrance industry and those located in California. It was a festive affair, and the exhibition was a hit with the press and the attendees. On the occasion of the opening of the museum and exhibition, the mayor of Los Angeles presented me with a proclamation While I was in Los Angeles, I was also invited to be the keynote speaker at a luncheon hosted by Beauty Industry West and was presented with the first annual Legend of Beauty Award.

FIDM continues to feature a permanent venue for the museum and creates revolving presentations from the collection on the main campus, as well as at three other locations of the college: San Francisco, Orange County, and San Diego. Press materials confirming FIDM's commitment stated, "The three-prong purpose of the Annette Green Perfume Museum includes an outreach program which would be inspirational for the fragrance industry, the public, and academia."

Unfortunately, Robert Nelson, my enthusiastic collaborator, unexpectedly retired a few years after the opening of the museum. His absence left its future rather hazy. Yet, there it remains, ensconced in its cozy space, the only perfume museum in the United States.

As I write this, it occurs to me that this is the perfect time for FIDM and the industry to consider creating a virtual perfume museum, which could be enjoyed by enthusiasts around the world. Now that's a project to run with!

---

1. A New York contingent was led by Marc Rosen (director of the exhibition and vice president of design and communication, Elizabeth Arden) and his glamorous wife, Arlene Dahl. Board members included Eugene Milano, president, Dana Perfumes; James Bosek, executive vice president, Houbigant; and Raymond Baliatico, president, Prince Matchabelli. Also on hand for the celebration were John and Sally Ledes, *Beauty Fashion*; Marilyn Miglin; Sherry Baker, Erno Laszlo Institute; Billie Sutter, *Elle* magazine; Christie and Ed Lefkowith, private lenders to the exhibition; John Triggle and Anna Galiani, Givaudan; Leslie Weller, Elizabeth Arden; and Melisande Congdon-Doyle, *Harper's Bazaar*.

2. Fragrance suppliers were led by Fragrance Resources in cooperation with Camili, Albert & Laloue, Dragoco, Drom International, Givaudan, Haarmann & Reimer, International Flavors & Fragrances, J. Manheimer, Mane USA, PFW, Pochet of America, Polarome, Quest International, Roure, and Takasago USA.

3. Chicago-based participants included Quintessence (formerly Jovan) and Marilyn Miglin.

4. I was joined on the receiving line at the gala preview by board member Kitty D'Alessio, vice chairman, new ventures and special projects, Chanel; Jeffrey N. Rudolph, administrative VP of the California Museum Foundation; Margo Scavarda, VP and divisional merchandise manager, fragrance and cosmetics of the Broadway, and chairperson of the retail committee of the *Scents of Time* exhibition; and Don M. Muchmore, executive VP of the California Museum Foundation and executive museum director of the California Museum of Science and Industry. The presence of Rose Marie Bravo (chairman of I. Magnin), Bob Mettler (CEO, Robinson's), and Michael Hecht (president of the Broadway) added to the excitement.

5. Geoffrey Beene, Bill Blass, Caesars World, Caron, Chanel, Christian Dior, Evyan, Max Factor, Fendi, Giorgio of Beverly Hills, Givenchy, Guerlain, Calvin Klein, Karl Lagerfeld, Parfums Stern, Jean Patou, Revlon, Nina Ricci, and Elizabeth Taylor's Passion.

6. Supporting retailers included Ann Gravseth, merchandise manager, cosmetic, JCPenney; Tom Sharp, general manager, Saks Fifth Avenue; Sanford Sachs, senior vice president and general manager, Marshall Field's; and Dr. Maria Clinton Battles, Parfumerie Marie Antoinette.

V

Tango to Higher Ed

Favorite Co-conspirators

Estelle Ellis, president, Business Image, and consultant, FIT
Shirley Goodman, executive vice president and executive director, Educational
    Foundation for the Fashion Industries, FIT
John Ledes, publisher, *Beauty Fashion*
Dean Jack Rittenberg, School of Business, FIT
Professor Peg Smith, chairperson, Bachelor of Science Degree Program, FIT
Lawrence Aiken, president of Sanofi Beauté and chairman of the Fragrance
    Foundation board
Burt Tansky, president, Bergdorf Goodman
Dr. Joyce Brown, president, FIT

Part 1—Tango Trumps

*Annette Green climbed onto the stage in the grand ballroom
of the Waldorf Astoria Wednesday night and did a tango. She
had a good reason to dance. More than 1,250 executives from
the beauty and fashion industries were there to honor her for her
thirty-two years as head of the Fragrance Foundation.*
—*Women's Wear Daily,* **October 22, 1993**

W hen the Fashion Institute of Technology (FIT) chose me to be the
1993 honoree at its ninth annual gala, "One Person Makes the

Difference,"[1] I was thrilled. What I didn't know, however, was that there were plans afoot to have me dance the tango in front of an audience of over a thousand of my peers. The idea was triggered by the hit movie of the moment, *Scent of a Woman*. Al Pacino and Gabriella Anwar starred in the film and caused a sensation when they performed what was described as a "spectacular tango."

To be certain I wouldn't make a fool of myself, FIT offered to foot the bill for one week of tango lessons. I have always enjoyed dancing and in the fifties even won a first-place trophy in a rumba competition. I felt the tango was quite another story, however. I lucked out. My tango teacher turned out to be the very patient and talented Pierre Dulaine of the American Ballroom Theater. We worked for about three hours every evening in his studio, and I practiced another hour or so at home.

When the big moment arrived a week later, my nerves were raw. I felt unbelievably shaky and uncertain I could pull it off. Fortunately, Mr. Dulaine agreed to be my on-stage partner, which certainly gave me a lot more confidence. I knew he would make me look good whatever happened. I wore a long black Spanish-lace gown to add to the illusion that I knew what I was doing.

Once I was on stage, my heart began to beat wildly. As we started to dance, the most remarkable thing happened: The industry members in the audience began to stamp their feet in unison. For some unfathomable reason, the rhythmic sound acted as a security blanket. I threw myself into the dance and finished to a standing ovation. I laughed to myself when my colleagues later raved about what an accomplished tango dancer I was. I can assure you I was more than happy to slip back into my favorite role as cheerleader for the industry.

Another fun highlight of the evening was when gala chair, Lawrence Aiken, joined with his co-chair, Burt Tansky, to rattle off a riff comparing my take on fragrance with a group of history's notables—from Cleopatra and Marie Antoinette to Sir Walter Raleigh and Napoleon. They ended their script by proclaiming, "Thanks to the fragrance industry's unsinkable Molly Brown, fragrance has become a universal language and the essence of our global economy."

Later in the evening, Mr. Aiken was honored with the Fashion Industry of Technology's Distinguished Advocate award. In his gracious acceptance remarks, he paid me another great compliment. "Green," he said, "was responsible for turning fragrance into an international economic success."

Afterglow

Oscar de la Renta, my dinner partner at the gala, sent me a double-framed memento with a picture of us on the left facing his handwritten note:

I was honored and happy to be next to you at your great evening! I am sure this was a night you will never forget. I was really glad to be a part of it.

The gala generated over $900,000. It became the financial impetus for the university to create the first bachelor of science degree program in America with a major in cosmetics, fragrances, and toiletries marketing. The monies also made it possible to develop what was to become the Annette Green/Fragrance Foundation Studio.

By establishing a fragrance laboratory, FIT gave students a career edge. They would learn firsthand about essential oils, how fragrances are developed, constructed, evaluated, and tested. The studio was designed by Ricky Pang, facilities designer at the college, after I arranged for his visits to the fragrance laboratories of several of the Fragrance Foundation's supplier members. He also met with leading perfumers. The 980-square-foot studio included ten workstations and an odor-free evaluation room for testing products. A number of the suppliers provided a sourcing guide for the necessary equipment, ingredients, and supplies. Beautiful factices (giant display reproductions) of famous perfume bottles were also contributed. The studio was in full operation for the fall '94 semester. By the spring, a mini course educated students on the basics.

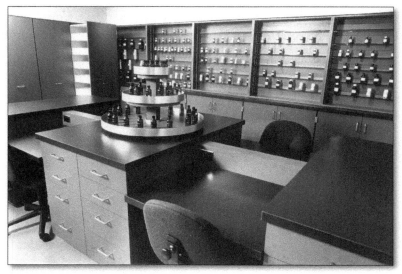

Annette Green/Fragrance Foundation Studio at FIT.

FIT established two perpetual scholarships to aid students in the program who achieved a 3.0 GPA at the end of their junior year. One was in my name alone, and the other I shared the honor with Robert Chavez, president, Hermès.[2] It has been a joy each year to meet the students who earned scholarships and are destined to become dedicated beauty-industry careerists.

In 1994, I received a related and much appreciated honor at a SUNY banquet in Washington, D.C., as the first industry leader to be recognized by FIT with its One Person Makes the Difference Award.[3] At the time, I was a member of FIT's educational board and in discussion about the possible development of a master's degree program in cosmetics and fragrance management.

In 1996, the Fashion Institute of Technology took the first step. An exploratory committee was formed under the direction of Bruce Chambers, dean of the graduate school at FIT. Peg Smith, chairperson of the bachelor of science degree program, and I were invited to join. Representatives from the administration and other departments in the university all participated.

The goal of the new master's degree program was to target outstanding talent already employed in the cosmetics and fragrance industry. Classes would be offered in summer and evening sessions. Much of the instructional content was to be available through the internet to allow students called away on business to maintain a synchronous communication with their instructors and classmates. As part of their library privileges, students would also have access to specialized research materials and other resources available on the internet.

FIT was the first educational facility in America to develop this field of study for graduate students. Designed to provide advanced managerial and marketing education for general and marketing managers in the cosmetic and fragrance world, the program curriculum was conceived to encompass three content areas. The first of these areas would address such managerial competencies as communication and presentation skills, leadership, and strategic planning. The second area was to focus on general managerial knowledge in the areas of market research, marketing communications, corporate finance, and global trade. And the third would delve into industry-specific subjects such as the history of the industry, product knowledge and development, packaging design, and management.

At an industry luncheon in the late nineties, Professor Peg Smith announced to everyone's delight that SUNY had approved the proposed master's degree program. Next came a search for an accomplished leader. It came to fruition with the appointment of Stephan Kanlian to serve as program director.

First-Class Affair

The first class of master's degree students were welcomed in fall of 2000. Initially, only twenty-five were accepted into the program. Today, Professor Kanlian is chairperson. Under his dedicated guidance, the program has expanded dramatically and is financially supported by leading companies in the beauty industry. The Estée Lauder Companies took an early leadership position with a $10,000 contribution.

Mastering the Art

The 2014 graduating class marked the program's tenth anniversary with a brilliantly conceived capstone research presentation. Backed by sophisticated, technically savvy visuals, the class members urged the industry to focus more strategically on the changes taking place in society, as well as in technology and consumer attitudes. Produced annually by the graduates, the program is presented in the FIT auditorium and attracts a broad-based audience, including beauty industry leaders. Among the underwriters present to celebrate the anniversary were Lever Brothers, Bath & Body Works, and Coty Beauty. Special awards were presented by each company to several outstanding students in a variety of honorary categories. A proud moment for all.

Part 2—Bold Beginnings

Annette became the driving force in the development of FIT's Cosmetic, Fragrance, and Toiletries program, and the impetus behind its expansion into a bachelor of science degree program. It is not just the first, but the only, academic program of its kind in the world. And it stands alone as a role model for business/education alliances.

—Dr. Allan F. Hershfield, president of
Fashion Institute of Technology

As I write this, twenty-five years have rushed by since the bachelor's degree in cosmetic, fragrance, and toiletries marketing was established. The program has graduated twenty-five students each year, and more than 80 percent have been employed by the fragrance and beauty industry. Happily, the number keeps growing.

My involvement with the Fashion Institute of Technology (FIT) began in the early eighties, when I became concerned about the lack of young people, particularly women, being prepared to enter the beauty industry in executive positions. Opportunities were limited, and few were aware of them anyway. Those job seekers who wandered in or were placed by a personnel agency usually found themselves hired as secretaries, receptionists, salesgirls, or makeup artists. Many, including me, were there by chance.

I had met and worked with late, great Shirley Goodman in the early eighties. A SUNY college, FIT in those days was understandably focused on the basics of fashion: design, merchandising, and patternmaking. The curriculum was obviously geared to the needs of the New York fashion industry. Changes were afoot, however, that revealed a burgeoning role for fashion as a synonym for style and beauty well beyond ready-to-wear. Products—from cars to toys and cosmetics to fragrances—were considered "fashion as lifestyle." I felt it was the perfect moment for me to start a conversation with FIT to address what was to become a major market marker. At the top of my list was the beauty industry, which was increasingly partnering with fashion designers. Licensing agreements were considered indispensable in the creation and marketing of fragrances.

A joyous moment greeting students in the Bachelor's program.

I asked Shirley Goodman if we could set up an appointment to talk about a proposal I was eager to make. She invited me to her office. Once there, I forged ahead, explaining my belief that the university could play a major role in response to growing interest by a broad spectrum of businesses in capturing the imagery of fashion as a marketing tool for a wide variety of categories. I suggested the possibility of FIT taking a leadership position in developing curriculum that would address a cross-section of industries. Of course, my priority was fragrance and beauty. They afforded an easy entry for an existing segment of the student body who were not necessarily committed to a career in fashion from a traditional perspective. Shirley was not sure I was right, but was willing to establish a not-for-credit elective in cosmetic and fragrance marketing. The only caveat was that she wanted me to teach the course myself one afternoon a week. I had to say yes.

I quickly found myself knee-deep in student affairs. The challenge was to act fast and stitch together a concept that would help students understand the structure and career potential of the beauty industry. I focused their attention on the industry's idiosyncrasies, terminology, and important players. The next step was to develop a curriculum that would inspire participation, be imaginative, and share as much professional knowledge as possible. I divided my first class of twenty-five students into five teams. Each was asked to build a marketing/promotion/public relation strategy around a product currently on the market. They were encouraged to contact beauty and/or fragrance companies to obtain whatever background materials and product samples they might need. The students on each team had to select a major city and retailer in which they wanted the product to be sold. A key element of the project was to imagine a tie-in with an important local charity for which a fund-raising event would be developed. It was the responsibility of the students to research and create a profile based on the personality of the city of their choice, as well as the charity, which had to include the actual names and addresses of contacts.

As soon as all the facts were gathered, the class was ready to move forward with a letter-writing campaign to everyone involved. The letters had to clearly and concisely detail the promotional events and outline how they would translate into maximum in-store excitement and attract media coverage. Each team was responsible for providing a theme for the promotion that would work in stores, windows, and at the counter, as well as at the charity event.

To give the whole effort a real-world focus, each team had to create an onstage presentation at the end of the semester. Representatives from the companies that the students had selected to feature, as well as editors from the beauty industry's leading trade publications, were invited to attend and judge the entrees.

The students not only rose to the occasion but developed wonderfully professional materials to illustrate their strategies. Each team chose to dress in color-coordinated outfits that reflected its theme and the materials that were exhibited. At the conclusion of the presentation, the enthusiastic reaction of the audience made it was clear that the class had "pushed the ball over the line." At this point, audience members were asked to judge the presentations. We tabulated the results and announced first-, second-, and third-place winners.

The program was off and running and created quite a buzz in the corridors of FIT. In fact, I was asked to meet with several of the department heads at the university. They were eager to learn how to liaise with industries in their fields of expertise, which could have a similar payoff. Today, it is a given. FIT has become an indispensable hybrid in preparing students for successful careers in far-flung fields throughout the global business community.

Backstage Strategy

It wasn't long before overwhelming student interest inspired expansion plans for the fragrance curriculum.

That's when I received a call from the late, vivacious dean, Jack Rittenberg. He wanted me to help him put the machinery in motion to develop an evening course that would be available to students as an elective. What he needed most was a qualified person to oversee the effort. I immediately thought of Hazel Bishop (a chemist and inventor of the indelible lipstick). Hazel and I had been friends and colleagues over the years. She had suffered a number of reversals in her career. At the time, she was associated with a small investment company as the in-house cosmetic industry guru. I had helped her gain new visibility within the industry as a participant in our annual state of the industry panel discussions.

My goal was to give her the opportunity to meet Dean Rittenberg in a setting that would appear to be serendipitous. I decided to have her sit next to him at the dinner following the upcoming FiFi Awards ceremony. I can only report that, by the time dinner was over, the deed was done, and when the fall semester started, Hazel was on staff and in charge of developing the course. It wasn't easy, since there was no precedent and a very small, insignificant budget. She struggled to prevail. She did.

By the time Hazel stepped down—to be succeeded as chairperson by Peg Smith in 1996—the program was enjoying great success and had morphed into a two-year bachelor of science degree. Peg took the fledging effort to new heights. She was a fabulous partner, and together, we deepened the involvement of beauty industry members. They were particularly enthusiastic about a mentorship program we had developed. Their participation as mentors became critical to the success of the students. We also involved key players from the fragrance and beauty world to participate in the Cosmetics/Fragrance Action Council, which I had established and chaired. Meetings were held regularly to set directions for the program, review changes to the curriculum, and established fund-raising goals. Monies raised assisted needy students, provided necessary materials for study, and funded an annual trip to Europe for qualified students. The trip

Left to right, Dr. Jack Mausner, Senior Vice-President, Research and Development, Chanel, me, Shirley Goodman, Executive Vice President and Executive Director of the Educational Foundation for the Fashion Industries, F.I.T., and Arthur Reiner, Chairman and Chief Executive Officer of Macy's Northeast.

offered a rare opportunity to see for themselves how flowers for perfume are cultivated and processed. They viewed the perfumer's art of creation and observed marketing and sales techniques in France and England. It was the chance of a lifetime to experience the depth and breadth of what makes the industry tick globally.

Fund-raising to benefit the bachelor's program at FIT in the most positive and enjoyable way possible became a priority. I began to think about the possibility of connecting it in some way to the Fragrance Foundation's FiFi Awards ceremonies. I proposed to a committee of industry leaders, including the dynamic Herb Morris and the legendary publisher John Ledes, that we consider holding post-awards luncheons. My plan was to salute the previous night's winners and runners-up each year. Everyone agreed it would also be meaningful to honor two prestigious members of the fragrance industry, who would be selected by the committee.

The concept was quickly embraced, and the members agreed to participate in an advisory capacity. We all agreed on the importance of selecting a unique award for the industry honorees. Thanks to Cartier, we certainly got it: a stunning crystal trapezoid design. The annual luncheons, which were also sponsored by Cartier (with special appreciation to Simon Critchell, Joseph Giugliano, and Robert Filotei) became an overnight success and the centerpiece of Fragrance Week in New York. Everyone wanted to attend. The program was developed in cooperation with the Action Council.

Monies were raised each year to support scholarships for the study-abroad program. By the tenth annual luncheon, thirteen students won grants totaling $49,800.

The guiding hand for the program today is a talented and dedicated woman, Virginia Bonofiglio, chair of the cosmetics and marketing bachelor's program. Her credentials as a perfumer make her an unqualified inspiration for the students.

Honors Galore

A celebration of the twenty-fifth anniversary of the bachelor's program was held at the elegant New York Yacht Club at the beginning of 2014. Four outstanding alumnae were honored: Tennille Kopiasz, Coty Prestige; Orrea Light, L'Oreal Paris; Bettina O'Neill, Barneys New York; and Shaunda Swackhamer, Estée Lauder Companies. The magnificent award, designed and created by FIT professor and sculptress Wendy Yothers, was presented to each honoree by Professor Peg Smith and me. The young women, poised and eloquent, certainly impressed the over two hundred members of the beauty industry in attendance.

The ceremony was opened with remarks by the charismatic Dr. Joyce Brown, president of the Fashion Institute of Technology, and the awards presentation was emceed by Jenny Fine, editor of *Beauty Inc*. Thanks to the generosity of underwriters Barneys New York, the Estée Lauder Companies, Mane, Coty Prestige, Firmenich, Gurwitch Products, and L'Oreal Paris, and the sellout attendance, the anniversary celebration was financially successful too. Virginia Bonofiglio participated in the ceremonies benefitting the Bachelors Cosmetics and Fragrance Marketing Scholarship Fund and the Annette Green/Fragrance Foundation Studio. Happily for everyone involved, the studio was dramatically expanded and redesigned several years ago as part of a major building initiative developed under the leadership of President Brown. It now can accommodate many more students and also offer hands-on training in developing cosmetic formulae.

On a scale from one to ten, I have to say talking Shirley Goodman into allowing me to develop a course in cosmetic/fragrance marketing way back in the early eighties was way off the scale. Maybe a twenty!

---

1. The woman behind the creation of the award I was to receive was the late Estelle Ellis, a renowned marketing legend in her own time. President of Business Image, she had also been a consultant to the Fashion Institute of Technology Foundation for many years. It was she who proposed me as the recipient of the 1993 One Makes the Difference Award because of my breakthrough work in olfactory science, as well as my leadership in the fragrance industry.
2. Mr. Chavez, president, Hermes USA.
3. In the June 1994 issue of *Mirabella* magazine, I was named one of "America's 1,000 Most Influential Women."

VI

Divine Beauté Divine

The most wonderful inspirations die with the subject, if he [or she] has no hand to paint them to the senses.
—**Ralph Waldo Emerson**, *Essays*

My fascination with the global business of scent led me to visit many grand parfumeries around the world. None, however, was more inspiring than the exquisite Beauté Divine on the Rue Saint-Sulpice on the Left Bank in Paris.

Lovingly tended by Mme Regine de Robien, a legendary perfume aficionado, she was someone I was determined to meet. The opportunity presented itself one bitter-cold winter day in the eighties. I had a letter of introduction and was full of anticipation as I approached her shop. Inside, I found a perfume lover's dream, filled with endless displays of exquisite bottles and boxes. Gently lit, the space held a mix of head-spinning elixirs. It was like walking into a cathedral dedicated to the eternal beauty and allure of the senses.

After we shared our mutual love of the beauty world, Mme de Robien invited me to see a special treasure trove that was under lock and key in a room below the shop. It held rare perfume bottles that were scheduled to be offered at an upcoming auction. She warned me it was very cold down there and that I should keep my fur coat on. She put on hers, too, and down we went through an entrance next to Beauté Divine shop. As we descended the stairs, it was like stepping back into revolutionary France. Ancient massive stone walls surrounded us. Finally, we reached an impressive steel door. Mme de Robien held a large brass key and dramatically pushed it into the lock. Once the door was open, she turned on the lights. There before me were about eight rows of industrial shelving filled to the brim with a mélange of fabulous historic bottles holding hints of rare perfumes worn a very long time ago. One alluring (and expensive) bottle of men's cologne, resembling the grillwork of an early Rolls-Royce, caught my eye and tickled my fancy.

As I walked through the heatless room ogling each bottle and box, I found myself getting colder and colder. So did Mme de Robien, who, after assessing the situation, asked if I would like some champagne to "warm us up." I certainly did not resist.

"I will be right back," she announced and, with key in hand, left me, locking the door behind her. I wasn't thrilled with the prospect of being abandoned in the freezing room, but wrapped my fur tighter around me and waited for what seemed like a lot more than the eight minutes it actually was. I was very happy to hear Mme Robien unlocking the door. She peeked in and explained she would open the champagne in the hall to be sure the popping cork didn't hit and break any of her treasures. She closed the door again but, happily, didn't lock it this time. In a moment or two, she returned with a magnum of champagne and two glasses, which she proceeded to fill with the much anticipated bubbly warm-up. We sat on two wooden folding chairs wrapped in our coats and toasted the success of the upcoming auction.

It was a heady moment that I recall with great relish.

I also had the pleasure during that trip to Paris to visit a Nina Ricci facility located in Ury, about thirty miles from the City of Light. It was an imposing two-story glass-walled structure with breathtaking views of the countryside. Inside, women in a colorful variety of chic pastel-colored uniforms were seated at individual work stations polishing the L'Air du Temps perfume flacons by hand and artfully tying gold threads around the necks of the sealed bottles topped by the famous double-dove stoppers. After viewing these artisans at work, I was escorted upstairs to visit Robert Ricci's office.[1] It was awesome. An elegant Louis XIV desk sat in the center of the handsomely furnished room surrounded by impressive paintings, perfectly stacked books, and of course, perfume bottles.

As I glanced around the office and looked out the picture window at the exquisite view, I asked my guide how often Mr. Ricci visited. "Once or twice a year," he revealed.

My immediate response: "How sad!"

He quietly countered, "Madam, beauty is never wasted."

Yet another priceless lesson in the seen and unseen pleasures of sensory awareness.

A moment with Robert Ricci.

Midnight Magic

One of the most provocative and trendsetting beauty events I was ever invited to attend was held in Paris on December 21, 1996. The longest day of the year, it heralded the opening of the Sephora cosmetic and fragrance boutique on the Champs-Élysées. The riotous all-night affair kicked off at midnight and was beamed through closed-circuit television to Sephora stores across France. The dream of Dominique Mandonnaud, who bought Sephora in 1993, was to give customers the pleasure of discovering and interacting with a vast assortment of fragrances and beauty products openly displayed on floor-to-ceiling shelves. It was a major step in releasing perfumes and cosmetics from their "prison" behind locked counters and glass doors.

The all-night party was the talk of Paris. Kleig lights, set up on the street in front of Sephora, drew throngs. A bright-red Hollywood-style carpet ran from the sidewalk right through the tunnel-like environment. Enthusiastic guests, including French fashion designers, industry leaders, and most surprisingly, the public, happily walked the carpet to no one knew where. It was a sensory spectacle.

Toward the back of the store, a stage setting revealed camera crews set up to capture the excitement and provide a theatrical area for interviews with visiting VIPs and, most important, the fashion designers whose fragrances were on display. I remember the charge of electricity when the provocative designer Jean Paul Gaultier arrived with his entourage. They sandwiched an interview with me in between M. Gaultier and other fashion stars. I took advantage of the opportunity to share news of the Fragrance Foundation, as well as fragrance happenings in the States.

One of the attractions that crowds of curious observers stopped for was a specially constructed perfumer's organ built in the round.[2] Hundreds of small brown laboratory bottles, filled with fascinating elixirs from the natural and scientific worlds, were available to reveal their contents to eager noses. Strategically located just inside the store, it was staffed by perfumers from the fragrance supplier Quest, who explained and demonstrated how the great perfumers conjure up the most magical scents from these disparate smell sensations.

Champagne and hors d'oeuvres were served to the surging crowd that filled every inch of the store all night long. A disc jockey kept a loud and forceful beat going around the clock. Speaking of clocks, when I departed sometime in the middle of the night, I was presented with the most exquisite sphere-shaped perfume bottle created to commemorate the evening. The crystal globe-shaped flacon was topped by a brilliant sapphire-blue glass stopper in the shape of the hands of a clock set to five minutes past midnight. The signature of the renowned artist/perfume bottle designer Serge Mansau was inscribed in gold against a midnight-blue background on the bottom of the weighty flacon. A sprinkling of gold stars strewn across the outer surface added to its lush and romantic appeal.

When I returned to New York, I spoke to many of my colleagues in retail and public relations about the extraordinary store but was met with a surprising lack of interest. Nevertheless, a retail revolution was about to take place that was still unknown in the United States. (It has been reported that the Paris-based Sephora has had more visitors since its debut than the Eiffel Tower.) Sephora was poised for global glory when LVMH acquired the chain in 1998.

The American beauty industry's take, however, on the 1999 opening of the first Sephora shop on Fifth Avenue at Rockefeller Center in New York was, to say the least, skeptical. Few were convinced such a concept could succeed. It was true that the initial efforts to duplicate the Champs-Élysées self-serve merchandising environment were flawed, mostly because of the store's three-level uninviting layout.

Time, however, has been on Sephora's side, and a variety of changes were made to accommodate the US market. Today, there are approximately four hundred imaginatively designed stores across the country. They have proved to be highly credible and successful competitors. There is little doubt that Sephora is now one of the beauty world's retail stars.

---

1. In the late seventies and eighties, Mr. Ricci and I enjoyed a staunch fragrance friendship. We shared our passion for perfume and most especially, the historical treasure trove of the fragrance world. "The creation of perfume is no ordinary act, but an act of love" was his oft-quoted mantra. Touché! When Mr. Ricci died in 1988, I was invited to speak at his memorial. It was an honor I still cherish.

2. A perfumer's organ (think of a miniature version of the magnificent Radio City musical attraction) was the workspace of the fragrance industry's creative "noses" in the early twentieth century. It was built in a half circle, with a dozen or more shelves holding hundreds of vials filled with precious essential oils and the latest synthetic discoveries. The perfumer, like a composer visualizing musical notes, sat in front of the organ and selected individual bottles to smell and identify. His final choice was based on a myriad of notes housed in his (or her) memory bank, which were then blended into a new fragrance accord.

VII

China on the Edge

Favorite Co-conspirators

Murray Pearce, editor, London trade paper, *Cosmetic News*
Sally Yeh, president of Bijan Fragrances and board member of the Fragrance
    Foundation

*Look in the perfumes of flowers and nature for peace of mind
and joy of life.*

                               —Wang Pei,
                             Tang Dynasty Poet

I was invited to go to China in the mid-eighties (the year before the Tiananmen Square debacle) by my good friend and colleague Murray Pearce. The editor of a London trade publication, he also served as a member of the board of the UK Fragrance Foundation committee, which produced its own version of the FiFi Awards. An extraordinary man, I admired him personally as well as for the scope of his dedication to the fragrance industry. In fact, it was Murray who worked with me hand in hand in the early nineties to establish the UK Fragrance Foundation.

History Revisited

I joined a prestigious group of fragrance and cosmetic executives, including Sally Yeh. We were all going to China to participate in a major international conference in Beijing organized by the Ministry of Light Industry of the

People's Republic of China and the International Federation of Essential Oils and Aroma Trades. Murray, one of the organizers of the conference, invited me to be a keynote speaker. I dedicated my remarks to the history of fragrance development and appreciation in China.

The Fragrance Foundation library was, as always, a trove of fascinating information, allowing me to detail China's remarkable fragrance history. The audience included several hundred industry members from China and Europe. As it turned out, few of China's representatives knew much about their own fragrance history.

Among the books I turned to was one of my favorites: *In Search of Perfumes Lost* by Paolo Rovesti:

If there is a country in which perfumes have an original elected homeland of their own, that country is China, which had such a predilection for them and enhanced them not only *from* the point of view of olfactive pleasure, but especially of the spirit. For a Chinese (and I refer to lost perfumes and hence to the Chinese of that time, gone with their perfumes) fragrances signified a state of the mind and had the capacity to speak like a language and create harmonies of mood.

Other research revealed that perfume, in incense form, played a major role in religious ceremonies, in food preparation, and in the home. Because water was suspect, washing garments (or even oneself) was simply not done. Kimonos were refreshed by hanging them on upside down U-shaped stands. Incense burners, placed in a space below the kimonos, allowed the fragrance to waft up and envelope and refresh the garments.

Different fragrance ingredients—flowers, roots, herbs, and spices, but most especially musk—were considered essential for the care and tending of the body, medically and psychologically.[1]

Chinese doctors considered these odoriferous ingredients to have healing properties. According to Paolo Rovesti, "If one counts the aromatic and perfume substances in China's ancient *Book of Medicine*, which still constitutes one of the most historic pharmacopies today, we find there are several hundred of them. The Chinese were the first to indicate perfumes as aromatherapeutic means. 'A perfume is always a medicine' is one of their maxims."

Even today, scores of people here and abroad look to these same ingredients to improve their well-being. In fact, it is rumored royal family members in England are devotees of Dr. Bach's Flower Remedies, and they are rarely sick.

I find it astounding and inspirational, too, to find my long-held convictions about the inherent artistry of fragrance basic to its history in China. "The Chinese were the creators of the earliest synesthetic: the mixer of multiple sensations: visual, auditive, and literary, which lifted the appreciation of a perfume to a plane of artistic elevation and greater spiritual involvement."[2]

Savoring the Sights

My visit to Beijing revealed a very different place then than it is now. Few cars—just boulevards filled with miles and miles of bicycles. People of every age were riding to work, to school, to the markets. As young women on bikes whizzed by, I couldn't help but notice their perfectly styled haircuts. Most were wearing short black skirts and well-fitting white blouses. Each night as the temperatures dropped, however, huge bonfires were lit on street corners for people (mostly men) to huddle around.

Of course, we visited the Great Wall. Considered one of the wonders of the world, we enthusiastically began our climb. It was, however, no small feat. Each roughly hewn stone step was a different height, from very low to very high, and all the steps were covered with sand that blew in from the Gobi Desert. Very slippery. In fact, Sally Yeh did slip and hit the side of her face on the wall. That night, she looked as if she had been in a prize fight but, happily, was otherwise fine.

The day we went to the Wall turned out to be quite warm. Most of us were definitely overdressed. Fortunately, along the climb we met venders who were selling bottles of water. A modern and helpful touch, to say the least. I was feeling the strain of the climb and was just about to give up when I saw an ancient-looking woman on her way back down the steps. There was no way I could quit. I talked myself into going on. I am proud to report I made it to one of the destination levels. Slipping and sliding back down was another matter, but I did get some help, and I discovered a handrail.

We did all the other touristy things, including a tour of the Forbidden City and the Temple of Heaven, and of course, we enjoyed a traditional Peking duck dinner. Our group was supposed to fly to the Xi'an to see the renowned terracotta warriors, but at the last minute, the Chinese government decided not to allow us to go. Sadly, we were unable to have this decision reversed.

Magazine Madness

An unexpected and surprising event took place during our stay that involved the launch of the Chinese edition of *ELLE* magazine. My companions and I became aware of the sudden appearance of a crowd of men and very few

Sally Yeh, President of Bijan Fragrances and me.

women gathered around a group of models who were about to distribute copies of the first Chinese edition of the magazine. I am sure no one was prepared for what happened. In a split second, the crowd turned into a surging mob, pushing and shoving each other, hands outstretched to grab the magazine. As soon as the copies were gone—and they seemed to evaporate before you could count to ten—the crowd quickly dispersed, gratified with the success of their efforts. It was an astounding display of a pent-up desire to experience the glamour of the Western world. Fascinating, too, to see for ourselves how successfully and quickly China was moving to establish itself as an important emerging luxury marketplace. Obviously, the well-heeled Chinese are not staying put, either. Committed travelers, they are joining the ranks of global consumers as they discover the rest of the world.

Before we left Beijing, our delegation was invited to a formal dinner in the Great Hall of the People located just off the great expanse of Tiananmen Square. Each table was set with a large lazy Susan in the center that was constantly being refilled with food that was impossible to identify. I was not always sure what was being served. A representative of the conference organizers was seated next to me. His assignment, I gathered, was to guide my choices as each of an endless number of courses arrived. Talk about surprising sensory experiences! A gustatory challenge in any language.

Unseen Resolution

One of the interesting bits of information I picked up while I was in China had to do with the cultural revolution. Of course, everyone had to wear drab Mao suits, whether they liked them or not. To add insult to injury, women were forbidden to wear makeup or any other ornamentation. Perfume, however, saved the day in a small but significant way. Because it was invisible, women wore it without anyone being the wiser. It lifted their spirits and allowed them to express their femininity without getting into trouble. Brava! Brava!

> *"We are your virtues like perfumes,"* Confucius said, *"which bestow pleasure and beauty not only upon your heart but also upon that of others who know you."*
> **—Paolo Rovesti, In Search of Perfumes Lost**

Turning East

In the years since my trip, China has emerged as one of the world's dominant powers. Today, it offers the perfume world an increasingly important source of the essential oils that are being extracted from rare flowers, plants, and herbs. Many of the country's most exotic ingredients have given perfumers an expanded array of possibilities to add to their creative palettes. It is also no surprise that the increasingly affluent Chinese people are fast becoming fragrance devotees of globally popular scents. With a population of well over a billion (and on the rise), the future of fulfilling odoriferous desires appears to have no bounds.

---

1. Genders, Roy (1972). *Perfume Through the Ages*.
2. Rovesti, Paolo (1980). *In Search of Perfumes Lost*.

VIII

Advertising In and Out

Favorite Co-conspirators

Lawrence Aiken, president of Givenchy Parfums and Fragrance Foundation
    board member
Roy Elvove, brand manager, Saatchi & Saatchi

The trouble with the fragrance industry is that it thinks it is
selling product when, in reality, it is selling people.
                                    —Margaret Mead

There is definitely something to be said for an industry that is famous around the globe for its advertising savvy. Yet, almost without exception, it has been surprisingly reluctant to adopt a more vigorous, inventive public outreach linked to its roster of famous personalities, the glamorous annual awards ceremonies, the extraordinary research results linking fragrance to well-being, and the authority of the nonprofit Fragrance Foundation, which has long been dedicated to expanding consumer appreciation and enjoyment of the fragrance experience.

I have thought about the *why* a lot. Somehow or other, unlike music and film, the fragrance industry has never visualized itself on the world stage. Yes, it has definitely created a global demand for its products, but corporate marketing philosophy has prevented it from moving out into the limelight and being viewed as dynamic, thrilling, and experiential. It would require a dramatic shift to a new paradigm. So far, this has not been in the cards.

As an interesting aside, back in the eighties, the grand dame of fashion, Diana Vreeland, pithily observed, "I don't think fragrance ads are flirtatious enough. I think the industry is more into techniques of advertising than expressing the messages of the fragrance itself." I think she was (and is still) right.

What's more, there is a certain sameness about the advertising that really doesn't meaningfully differentiate one fragrance story from another. I am not suggesting that a company negate its individuality. Just the opposite. A good place to start would be with the FiFi. In my well over thirty years around the award winners, I have wondered why none of these companies has turned up the public heat by announcing the good news and giving consumers something to cheer about, olfactorally and psychologically speaking,

Imagine members of the movie and music business keeping their winnings to themselves. As everyone knows, it is perfectly normal for them to prime the pump by fanning out to every major market with ads announcing nominations and winners.

Of course, fragrance companies and their suppliers have traditionally run congratulatory ads in the industry's trade journals. But basically, that has been it. Because there has never had been a collective effort to prepare the public for the news of the nominees and, of course, the award winners, the FiFis remain a closeted industry affair.

The foundation tried to change this attitude over the years. We instituted a number of concepts, including a FiFi winner's seal that companies could include in advertising and affix to retail displays and packaging. Few ever used the seal. The industry has always been locked into its "reality" that winning a FiFi was an internal matter. How I wish that attitude would change.

As far as public service advertising is concerned, there was a moment back in the late eighties. Inspired by the highly successful generic milk industry's campaign, the board of the foundation approved the development of the industry's first national public awareness advertising theme "Stop and Smell the Memories." Board member Lawrence Aiken was the point person for developing the campaign with the foundation's staff. We worked with the agency of record, Saatchi &

Saatchi, to create the concept under the expert direction of the talented brand manager, Roy Elvove. It featured five different lifestyle situations based on a series of focus-group interactions we commissioned, as well as scientific information generated by the sensory psychologists funded by the Sense of Smell Institute. These studies more than confirmed the connection of memory to our fifth and least understood sense.

The campaign featured a series of full-page, two-color ads highlighting memorable situations being experienced by both sexes in a variety of age groups, from teens to forty-somethings. The campaign was presented to the publishers of magazine members of the foundation. They enthusiastically agreed to run the ads on a pro-bono basis for about a year.

The theme "Stop and Smell the Memories" inspired a National Fragrance Week contest in 1996. The Fragrance Foundation and the *New York Times* co-sponsored a special competition at fragrance counters in retail locations nationwide. Consumers were invited to share their favorite fragrance memories on special memory cards. Drawings were held at each location for prizes to be determined by retailers. The names of the grand-prize winners were sent to the Fragrance Foundation for a national drawing. A specially produced *Stop and Smell the Memories* video was available for in-store and local television use. It featured on-the-street interviewers posing questions related to scent and memories to enthusiastic passersby.

In spite of an excellent response by the public to the campaign, limited funding and support by the board and the industry presaged the beginning of the end. In recent years, yet another board of directors approved and produced a new public service ad campaign. It was still a no-go.

IX

Fragrance Fun Day Festivities

Favorite Co-conspirators

Jeanette S. Wagner, president of Estée Lauder International and chairman of
the Fragrance Foundation Board
Simon Critchell, president of Cartier Parfums
Donna Hanover, first lady of the city of New York and broadcast journalist

*You must fuse mind and wit with all the senses before you can
feel truth. And if you can't feel truth, you can't have any other
satisfactory sensual experience.*
—The Last Poems of D. H. Lawrence
The Viking Press, 1933

According to ongoing market research, consumers want to have more
fun! They haven't been getting much of it for years, either, as the
in-store shopping experience has become duller and increasingly stressful.
No wonder so many have turned to social media and the internet.

I first began to wrestle with the growing challenge back in the nineties.
It inspired me to develop Fragrance Fun Day. It turned out to be a wildly
successful disappointment. Why? Let me set the scene.

Our annual citywide fragrance festivities were in full swing. We had
the perfect venue for what we planned as a New York spectacular—the
mammoth tent at Lincoln Center. It was already rented for the day before
for the dinner following the FiFi Awards ceremony at Avery Fisher Hall.

Fun to be with New York City Mayor Ed Koch, Dr. Fernando Aleu and Richard
Lockman, President of Jean Patou.

The challenge was to mount a massive overnight cleanup in preparation
for the move-in of all the participants first thing in the morning. I put
a team in place to make it happen and dropped in through the night
to be sure everything was on a problem-free schedule. I was assured
all was well, though I have to say the scene was chaotic. I was used to
that, though, so I wasn't concerned. What no one told me was that the
sponsored banners, which were custom-made to decorate several double-
decker busses rented to shuttle attendees from various retail locations,
had not been placed in a secure area and were thrown away. I didn't learn
the ugly truth until an early morning phone call. I had to immediately
advise the underwriters: the Donna Karan Beauty Co., Aramis/Tommy
Girl, the Tova Corporation, and Condé Nast. Everyone was extremely
disappointed, but we all realized there was nothing we could do, and let
it go. The only saving grace was that aboard each bus, we were able to
feature the companies and their brand representatives, who entertained
passengers and distributed fragrance samples.

Fragrance Fun Day attracted over three thousand visitors who, as it turned out, came at the noon opening and stayed until eight o'clock closing time. We actually had to beg them to leave.

Donna Hanover joined me and Jeanette Wagner to cut the ribbon to launch the festivities.

Under sunny skies the balloon-bedecked tent at Lincoln Center was ready to welcome the public (men, women, and children) to the first festival ever to offer everyone sensory experiences they had never had before. Inside the big tent, visitors discovered a variety of colorfully decorated areas offering fun-filled interactive activities. They had the opportunity to create their own individual fragrances at the Firmenich Perfumery boutique, with the help of top perfumers. They explored living flower technology at the International Flavors & Fragrances Greenhouse and learned the latest in fragrance online technology from Quest International experts. Givaudan-Roure created a simulated Costa Rican children's fragrance rain forest. Parents joined their children on the tour and discovered the company's Scent Trek fragrance-capturing technology.

Avon built an antique perfume bottle boutique where experts were on hand to identify the history of bottles from anyone's personal collection. Perfumers from three fragrance suppliers—H&R, Florasynth, and Creations Aromatique—offered personalized fragrance makeovers. There were three outposts dedicated to fragrance horoscope readings sponsored by Estée Lauder USA and *Self* and *Mademoiselle* magazines.

An "open-air" theater was center stage in the tent. We dubbed it "Stars on Stage." Throughout the day, visitors were treated to live interviews with popular fragrance and fashion designers, celebrities, beauty editors, and newscasters. Participants included fashion designers Oleg Cassini, Oscar de la Renta, Nicole Miller, Josie Natori, and Mary McFadden. The *New York Post* gossip columnist Cindy Adams; French stage and nightclub performer Lilliane Montevecchi; fragrance creator and QVC regular Tova Borgnine; and China's influential beauty spokeswoman Yue-Sai Kan all made special appearances. Actress Arlene Dahl, known for her forays into the world of astrology, gave fragrance readings. Questions were taken during lively exchanges with the audience. After each session, drawings for fragrance prizes created quite a sensation.

A mock movie theater showed films and videos starring the stories of how fragrance was made and how the world and nature contributed to fragrance creation, the history of fragrance featuring the *Scents of Time* exhibition video and other fascinating fragrance-related subjects.

Free tickets to attend Fragrance Fun Day were available at retail stores throughout the city. The Fragrance Foundation also distributed tickets to women's clubs, New York's Visitors Bureau, and other special locations.

A full-page ad announcing the festivities appeared in the *New York Times* on the Sunday before Fragrance Fun Day, and twenty-five thousand Fragrance Fun Day brochures were inserted into an equal number of Monday's home delivery editions of the *New York Times*. *New York* magazine also ran the ad in two issues, and Time Warner City Cable featured a thirty-second commercial during a ten-day period leading up to Fragrance Fun Day. A van from radio station WBLS parked on-site to cover all the happenings.

Retail partners included Barneys, Bloomingdale's, Century 21, Cosmetics Plus, Crabtree & Evelyn, Genovese, Lord & Taylor, Macy's, Nordstrom, Parfumerie Douglas, Perfumania, Rite Aid, Saks Fifth Avenue, Sterns, and Walgreen's. Fragrance Fun Day baseball caps, courtesy of GAP Inc., T-shirts underwritten by Avon Products Inc., and security wristbands provided by *New Woman* magazine were given to one and all.

At the board meeting following Fragrance Fun Day, we showed the members (most of whom had not attended) a terrific video recapping the excitement of the day. It definitely captured the magic. I reported the enthusiastic response of industry members who had not only participated but who, at the close of the day, indicated a commitment to a repeat performance the following year. Everyone agreed it was an ideal vehicle for reaching the public. Simon Critchell, a board member, proposed a series of Fragrance Fun Days be held in store parking lots across the country. Nevertheless, after evaluating the event, despite the overwhelming consumer appeal and long-term national potential, a review of the costs quickly negated the benefits, and in the blink of an eye, Fragrance Fun Day was history.

A practical decision or strategic mistake? We will never know, but it certainly was a *big* shock for everyone involved, including consumers and industry participants who kept calling, in vain, for information about plans for the following year.

Juggling in Japan

Favorite Co-conspirators

Yoshiharo Fukuhara, president of the Japan Cosmetic Industry Association
    and chairman of the board of Shiseido
Masabumi Sugawara, chairman of Japan Flavor and Fragrance Manufacturer's
    Association
Takio Yamada, managing officer, Office of Corporate Strategy and Planning
    of the international fragrance industry supplier Takasago International

> *Imagination is more important than* knowledge. *Knowledge is*
> *limited. Imagination encircles the world.*
> **—Albert Einstein, "What Life Means to Einstein,"**
> **interview in the *Saturday Evening Post*, 1929**

I was ecstatic to receive an invitation to visit Japan in the spring of 1997 from a
Mr. Yoshiharo Fukuhara and a Mr. Masabumi Sugawara. Not only was
I to be the guest of these leading organizations, but Governor Morihiko
Hiramatsu of the resort island of Oita, famous for its steam baths, also
invited me to visit its brand-new Musée de Parfum founded on the island
the year before.

From the minute I got off the plane in Tokyo, I was surrounded by
representatives of my hosts, who brought a phalanx of photographers
with them. Actually, I was not really up to facing cameras after such a
long trip but, of course, I did. Everyone showered me with the warmest

of greetings and bouquets of flowers, which quickly helped me forget the long and exhausting trip. It was the kind of reception I imagined was surely reserved for the most famous and favored inhabitants of this world. I relished every moment.

The Protocol of Bowing

The reception I received in Tokyo the next day was exceptionally cordial. I had not realized, however, what the protocol would be when it came to hosting an American woman executive. When I entered the conference room, I was greeted by a lineup of approximately fifteen male fragrance industry leaders waiting to welcome me. To deal with the gender question, I was introduced as "President Green," which made my acceptance as an honored guest so much more palatable than "Miss Green." I made my way down the line, bowing to each man who bowed back.

Before I had left New York, I had asked several of my colleagues about the tradition of bowing when meeting someone. I was advised to place the palms of my hands together in front of my body and bow from the waist.

Yours truly surrounded by members of the Japan Cosmetic Industry Association.

They were wrong. I belatedly found out that women bow with their hands at their sides. I learned the hard way when I discovered during a meeting break that several of the attendees were laughingly imitating my incorrect bow. When they saw me, they scattered to the winds. I immediately made the necessary change and went on to address the leading members of both industry associations. I was particularly touched by a very generous and enthusiastic introduction by Mr. Fukuhara. It meant a great deal to me, because this elegant man was considered one of Japan's most distinguished business leaders, innovators, and philanthropists. I was doubly honored.

Interest in the work of the Fragrance Foundation was at the core of my visit. Everyone was eager to explore how we might interact. Of course, the FiFi Awards were the center of attention, as was the breakthrough work of the Fragrance Foundation and the Olfactory Research Fund (later to be renamed the Sense of Smell Institute). During my presentations and meetings with the beauty press, I had the definite feeling that, despite the past lack of interest in fragrance (except as gifts and to be enjoyed in the bath), Japan was entering a new olfactory period and that the expanded use and appreciation of fragrance was part of this surprising development.

A Perfume Palace

The concerned and thoughtful guide who accompanied me throughout my trip was Mr. Takio Yamada. His warmth and wealth of knowledge added greatly to the success of my visit.

Mr. Yamada and I flew to Oita to visit the new perfume museum in the early morning. We were driven over rough, undeveloped roads for nearly an hour through a beautiful mountainous region. As the car wound its way up to our destination, we were surrounded by cherry blossom trees growing helter-skelter on the sides of the mountain like weeds. It was an amazing sight.

Finally, when we reached what felt like the top of the mountain, high above the clouds, an extraordinary edifice designed to honor the world of perfumery burst into view. Built in an elegant U shape, the two-story pink-brick building would have been perfectly at home at Versailles. A fountain and mammoth multicolored glass sculpture, an artist's interpretation of a flower's stamens, dominated the entrance of the courtyard that led to the museum. Inside, towering clear-glass walls provided a ravishing view of the cloud-filled mountains.

The museum itself was the repository of cultural treasures that traced the history of every facet of fragrance creation. A fascinating historical Japanese fragrance game room had been recreated. The museum had a theater and workrooms for visitors to learn how to make their own perfume and potpourri. Pierre Dinand, the brilliant French packaging designer (and creator of the FiFi award), had helped the museum director locate and acquire most of the historic perfume flacons and memorabilia. When I was there, a special exhibition of Pierre's many award-winning perfume bottle designs had been mounted in his honor.

One of the most appealing areas in the museum was a glass-enclosed greenhouse filled with the plants and flowers used in perfumes. The resident perfumer had everything he needed at his fingertips. The museum gift shop was particularly inventive. Never, never had I seen so many irresistible interpretations of fragrance and implements to use on the body and in every room in the home. Decorative wall hangings and crafts created by local artists were inspired.

That evening, I was the guest at an official dinner with the governor and staff members of the museum. He proposed that a special area be made available for a permanent exhibition featuring the work of the Fragrance Foundation. In addition, we talked about the possibility of making the focus of the 1998 Fragrance Week a city-to-city tribute between New York and Oita in appreciation of the Musée de Parfum. At the end of the evening, the governor presented me with a beautiful black lacquer vase. I embarrassed him by giving him a hug.

Back in Tokyo, I visited the breathtaking cherry blossom trees surrounding the palace moat, along with hundreds of Japanese residents and tourists. A festival was being prepared for that evening. It was a revelation to see how local office workers participated. In the early afternoon, many arrived with blankets, which they spread out to mark their reserved spaces. Each blanket was then overseen by one of the office workers who would be joined later in the day by colleagues who came loaded down with refreshments to enjoy as they all reveled in a light-and-sound show. An annual sensory extravaganza promoted by the city, I was eager to attend. Unfortunately, I had other commitments.

My next excursion was to Shizuoka via the Shinkansen (bullet train) to visit the Shiseido Perfume and Beauty Museum, which houses the history and scientific breakthroughs of the company—an inspirational experience. I was also received by Mr. Satoshi Suzuki, president and CEO of POLA Laboratories, where I viewed a beautiful collection of historical fragrance and cosmetic memorabilia.

Of course, while in Japan, I was eagerly looking forward to discovering the exquisite city of Kyoto. Arrangements had been made by Elizabeth Arden to have a guide meet me at the train station and to accompany me during my stay. He turned out to be a delightful young Brit who taught English when he wasn't moonlighting as a guide. What a treasure he was. He knew Kyoto like the palm of his hand. He not only showed me the exquisite old temples and all the wonderful tourist sights (including the geisha quarters) but arranged for me to accompany him to a private tea ceremony with a Buddhist monk who was a friend of his.

What a unique and, in many ways, surprising experience. I followed him along a narrow wooden walkway to a small structure that had to be entered through a very low doorway. Sitting opposite the entrance on a raised platform, with legs crossed in a lotus position, was a handsome young monk dressed in a light-salmon-colored kimono. He greeted my guide, who introduced me. We were asked to remove our shoes and sit cross-legged on the matted floor. Not easy. A man who was obviously the monk's helper brought us a special tea and cookies. A word about that tea: It was a very thick green concoction that I found undrinkable. I tried but was not too successful. The two men spoke about the ways of the world (my guide did the translations).

I was mesmerized by this religious man and kept totally focused on him. Since he was looking at me with great intensity, I felt that even though we were speaking through an interpreter, we were definitely in sync. As we got up to go, he asked my guide what I did. My guide explained that I was in the beauty business. The monk straightened out his arms to give him the leverage to lift himself up from his seated position and replied, "Tell her beauty is inside, not outside." I don't know what made him think I didn't know that. Guess I had not made such a meaningful impression after all.

I also can't forget accompanying my guide to the beautiful grounds of one of the famous temples of Kyoto. When we arrived, the gates were locked. As he tried to find out why, a nearby gate opened, and out poured several hundred men and women, all dressed in cotton work clothes (loose-fitting pants with matching overshirts). Each carried a broom and pail. They walked in unison to the locked gates, which were quickly opened, and disappeared inside. I was informed they were Japanese citizens who come to Kyoto from all over the country, annually, as volunteers to clean the sacred gardens. It was considered an honor to be allowed to participate. I certainly was impressed.

A year after I returned from Japan, the Fragrance Foundation was invited by Governor Hiramatsu to establish a permanent exhibition of FiFi winners at the Musée de Parfum. We proudly provided past and current winners. I was looking forward eagerly to even greater cooperation between the Musée and the foundation.

Unfortunately, when the infamous financial bubble broke in Japan at the beginning of the twenty-first century, tourists abandoned the spas on the island of Oita, and regretfully, many hotels and the museum itself were forced to close because of a lack of visitors. Even the governor was turned out of office. No one could have been sadder than I about the unfortunate turn of events, to say nothing of the loss of the exquisite perfume palace.

I met many charming and talented Japanese men and women wherever I went. They were all so cordial and eager to answer my questions and have me answer theirs. It added a lovely, unexpected dimension to the trip. For years we exchanged notes, pictures, and Christmas cards. Several colleagues visited me in New York. Most memorably, Mr. Yamada came to call on the morning of September 11. The purpose of his visit was to present me with an exquisite porcelain-faced doll dressed in a classic full-length red-and-gold floral-patterned silk kimono encircled with an obi at her waist. The obi closed dramatically with a full-blown bow at the back. The doll held an open fan in one of her delicate hands, and golden hair decorations were placed strategically throughout her jet-black wig. Standing fourteen inches tall, the doll was (and still is) protected under a large square Lucite cover. I was amazed she arrived intact. Happy (and grateful) as I was to receive such a beautiful gift, news of the sudden attack on the World Trade Center that unforgettable morning ended my colleague's visit in an atmosphere of confusion and dread. The doll is a poignant reminder that, despite the chaos surrounding her arrival, she is a calming presence, the essence of lasting beauty.

A visit with Takio Yamada.

XI

Certifying Success

Favorite Co-conspirators

Professor Peg Smith, chairperson, Cosmetics and Fragrance Marketing
    Bachelor's Program, Fashion Institute of Technology
Mary Ellen Lapsansky, vice president, the Fragrance Foundation
Mary Anne Havriluk, manager of fragrance online programs for Turnip
    Digital Inc.

All learning begins in the senses.

—Aristotle

always loved to interact with the salespeople who work behind the fragrance counters. I guess my commitment to these unsung heroes and heroines began when I first came to New York in the fifties and was hired by Richard Hudnut/DuBarry to write sales training materials. My inspiration was an insert in a book that Richard Hudnut had published in the late twenties, *The Romance of Perfume*. It was titled "At 20 Rue de la Paix," and it opened with a sensory bon mot:

> To trade in perfume is to belong to romance. Indeed, even in modern times there lingers much of the glamor and enchantment which have always clothed this business of distilling the essence of rare flowers into fragrance of magic charm.
>
> One goes into a perfumer's shop and feels instantly that one has slipped into an atmosphere of age-old mysteries and delights.

Even in some great, busy department stores the corner set apart for perfumes carries with it this sense of romance and expectancy.

Working under the tutelage of Christine Chiossi (see "Backstory" at the beginning of the book) made me aware of how important sales specialists were to the success of selling fragrance. The devotion of these behind-the-counter heroines touched my heart. Their total commitment to their brands, despite long hours on their feet, questionable appreciation, and next-to-nil opportunity to move up the ladder, was the envy of every other department.

In the early nineties, they inspired me to think about how the Fragrance Foundation could help. Working with my staff, we began a dialogue that led to the possibility of establishing a certification program to recognize and benefit sales specialists. We all agreed that it should be dedicated to giving these experts a broad-based variety of intellectual tools to increase their knowledge, as well as establish awareness and appreciation by the industry of their professionalism.

It was obvious that one of the challenges would be to develop a test based on a predetermined body of knowledge that the industry would respect and rally around. Everyone agreed the testing should focus on two major areas: the world of fragrance from a generic point of view (historical, cultural, and psychological) and the basic techniques of creative and successful selling.

We took the first steps to develop the structure in the fall of 1992 with Dade Perlov of the Consensus Management Group, specialists in a wide range of facilitation services and custom-designed program development.

To begin the process, focus groups were set up in New York, Minneapolis, Dallas, and Los Angeles. Their task was to generate input from prospective candidates on the certification curriculum. They also worked to spur interest and gain support of the certification program by management at retail and within the industry. The focus group participants included from twelve to fifteen top sales specialists from leading retailers. They met between September and December. A point person in each of the four major markets was chosen to aid in identifying testing sites, dates, and the sales specialist participants.

In the spring of 1994, a class of about a hundred sales specialists sat for the exam and became the first in their field to receive certified fragrance sales specialist (CFSS) certificates. Those who passed the proctored exam were also awarded specially designed pins engraved with the letters CFSS to wear as a badge of accomplishment for customers to see.

To qualify, a specialist was required to have worked in fragrance sales for at least two years and received a recommendation to work toward certification from his or her supervisor or vendor. The next step was to agree to prepare for the exam by studying the manual and other materials provided by the Fragrance Foundation. Once they submitted the necessary application and fee, they were eligible to be accepted by the independent certification board. The board was composed of several retailers and industry members and was chaired by Professor Peg Smith. The build was slow but steady, and by the third year, over 250 fragrance sales specialists had been certified.

The sales specialist who achieved the highest score on the examination each year was honored and flown to New York by the Fragrance Foundation to be recognized on stage at the FiFi Awards ceremony. She was also presented with an elegant Lalique vase. Heartfelt acceptance remarks by the yearly winner lent a deeply felt touch of reality to the ceremonies.

Over the years, the CFSS program morphed into a major internet opportunity for sales specialists around the world. The program, under the direction of Mary Ellen Lapsansky, made major strides in gaining global recognition and participation. By 2013, over thirteen thousand sales specialists had become certified. At this point, the CFSS master's program was introduced to benefit and recognize longtime members of this elite group.

Looking back at this important and uniquely successful effort, I am unsure what the future holds. As a matter of fact, I was contacted by Mary Anne Havriluk, manager of fragrance online programs for Turnip Digital Inc., at the suggestion of Mary Ellen. Ms. Havriluk reached out to me because her company planned to fill the void left by the discontinued Fragrance Foundation certification program which ended in 2013 after Mary Ellen's position was eliminated She particularly wanted me to write an introduction for the version that her company was producing. I did so after she sent me a copy of the complete program. It was extremely well done and could be of great help to sales specialists. I felt a definite twinge of regret that the Fragrance Foundation had surrendered this critical piece in the industry's sales training educational puzzle. It not only recognized the dedication of these behind-the-counter experts but, for the first time, gave them the confidence and in-depth insights to inspire their customers to have greater appreciation of the pleasures and emotional importance of fragrance.

Certification was not our first effort in providing behind-the-counter specialists with the enhanced tools to meaningfully communicate with the public. Way back in 1988, we developed the first "personalized fragrance analysis" kit. It represented a degree of fragrance professionalism usually only available to those selling skin treatment, makeup, and hair-care products. It was an early attempt in the foundation's evolution to expand educational opportunities for those stalwarts whose careers were dedicated to selling the importance of fragrance.

No one could question the independence and authority of the Fragrance Foundation. Our unbiased credentials had assured the success of the program from its bright beginnings to its ignominious end.

XII

Sense of Discovery

Favorite Co-conspirators

Richard Solomon, president, Charles of the Ritz

Dr. Jack Mausner, senior vice president, Research and Development, Chanel

Dr. Fernando Aleu, president of Puig of Barcelona and Fragrance Foundation board president

Dr. William Cain, neuroscientist, Yale Medical School

Dr. Robert Henken, neuroscientist, Georgetown Medical School

Alvin Lindsay, president of Roure and treasurer of the Fragrance Foundation

Henry Walter, president and CEO, International Flavors & Fragrances

Eugene Grisanti, executive vice president of International Flavors & Fragrances and Fragrance Foundation board member

Dr. Morley Kare, president, Monell Chemical Senses Center

Dr. Susan Schiffman, professor of medical psychology and director of weight-loss unit, Department of Psychology, Duke University Medical Center

Michael Sweeney, vice president of sales and marketing, International Flavors & Fragrances

Anthony J. Leardi, vice president, Fragrance Applications, Takasago International Corporation

Hans-Otto Schmidt, director, International Marketing, Haarmann & Reimer, GmgH

Susan Babinsky, business manager, Consumer Group, Kline & Company

Lewis Thomas, president emeritus of Memorial Sloan Kettering Cancer Center and chairman of the board of Monell Chemical Senses Center

From the senses originate all trustworthiness, all good conscience, all evidence of truth.
—Friedrich Nietzsche, Writings of Nietzsche, Volume 1

Way back in the early eighties, hardly anyone (me included) was aware of the importance of the senses in general and the sense of smell in particular. The science of brain mapping and its relationship to olfaction were still to come.

The most notable exception was the sensory-deprived icon Helen Keller. In fact, she referred to the sense of smell as the "fallen angel of senses," which it certainly was.

In his book *Helen Keller, Sketch for a Portrait*, published in 1956, the author, Van Wyck Brooks, wrote touchingly about Miss Keller:

> For her, the sense of smell was the most important aesthetic sense. She could usually tell by odors alone what part of a city she was in and saying that "there are as many smells as there are philosophies." She said that Fifth Avenue was a "very odorous street." She received olfactory impressions there of expensive perfumes, powders, and creams, choice flowers and delicate foods exhaling from the houses and, when a door was open, she knew what cosmetics were used within and whether they roasted their coffee and whether they used candles.

I was (and am) a longtime devotee of Miss Keller. Mr. Brooks's book had been in my library shortly after it was published. My wake-up call, however, didn't come until I read an article in the *New Yorker* about a laboratory at Yale under the direction of neuroscientist Dr. William Cain, who was doing deep-dive research into the sense of smell. I had no idea what to expect, but I called him up to ask. "Come up and see," he responded. I did. What a revelation! His studies, completely out of sight of the rest of the world, were dedicated to the human response to smells and their influence on our behavior.[1]

Rigorous Research

One of the projects I observed included a group of subjects, seated classroom style. In front of each person was a group of small paper drinking cups. The cups were stuffed with pieces of cotton impregnated with ordinary odors: Crayola, lead pencil, vanilla, and the fragrance ingredient jasmine. The subjects were asked to identify the smell sensations inside each of their cups. I was surprised, that without visual identification, this task turned out to be very difficult. After touring Dr. Cain's laboratory, I left Yale happy that I had found a kindred spirit and discovered a hidden inner sanctum devoted to smells.

My learning curve was about to grow exponentially when I heard about Dr. Robert I. Henkin, who was making news within the scientific community with his studies on the role of zinc and a healthy sense of smell. I called him, and he also invited me to visit his laboratory. He was extremely eager to share the details of his work. I was so impressed with his persona and expertise that after an hour or two, I invited him to speak at an upcoming seminar I was planning. He agreed. Over the coming months, he made several presentations, but I can't say they were totally appreciated (or understood) by the attendees. Nevertheless, these presentations began an exploration by the industry, spurred on by the Fragrance Foundation, into the mysteries of the sense of smell.

During that time, I discovered that Henry (Hank) Walter, head of the powerful perfume supplier company International Flavors & Fragrances, was totally committed to the scientific study of olfaction. As a matter of fact, he had established a laboratory full of sensory experts and chemists to spearhead the studies. When he heard of my growing involvement, he was more than encouraging. We began to meet regularly. He was very generous in sharing his knowledge. For me, it was the beginning of ever-increasing awareness of the unexplored world of olfaction.

My forays into the scientific community made me realize we were on the cusp of learning how dependent we all are on *how* and *why* we smell. Few in the fragrance industry, however, knew much about the olfactory system, and I can't say there was much interest.

Breaking Through

Nevertheless, I couldn't shake the feeling that our nonprofit educational organization, the Fragrance Foundation, should take a leadership position in developing and encouraging greater understanding of how the sense of smell operates and how odors influence our behavior.

The board of directors at the Fragrance Foundation was chaired by an incredibly knowledgeable and erudite Dr. Fernando Aleu. He was an immediate ally. The board met in 1980 to consider my proposal to create an independent, tax-exempt, charitable organization with the unique mission of exploring olfactory awareness and its potential influence on our sense of well-being. Several of the board members were reluctant to consider such a major undertaking, which they felt might result in information that could have dubious value.

After lengthy consideration, however, everyone agreed it was appropriate for the organization to play a part in opening the door to this most mysterious of all the senses. The hope, understandably, was that our efforts would have the potential not only to advance scientific understanding of smell but might result in greater appreciation and enjoyment of fragrance, as well as provide independent validation for product claims.

We had our lawyers register the new entity, the Fragrance Foundation Philanthropic Fund. A separate board was elected to administer and oversee the activities. The creation of the fund was approved by the state in 1981. The board elected Richard Solomon the fund's first president. A man of extraordinary commitment to our industry, Mr. Solomon made the first contribution to the fund of $5,000. Additional start-up contributions of $5,000 each were made by Jovan and the Fragrance Foundation.

The board's mission for the fund, as stated in the bylaws, was to "grant scholarships, sponsor scientific research, and promote the study of the olfactory arts and science; sponsor and conduct meetings, lectures and symposia; create programs and exhibits for libraries, art galleries, and museums; and develop public educational research that promotes and stimulates the study and understanding of our fifth sense; and solicit, receive, maintain, and disburse funds for these purposes."

The Talent behind the Talk

As we began our investigations into the field of sensory study, my research led me to Monell Chemical Senses Center in Philadelphia and to a long collaboration with its remarkable and talented leader, Dr. Morley Kare. Dr. Kare took me by the hand and led me through the labyrinth of his mysterious world. There, I met extraordinary young scientists whose lifework was devoted to the study of the sense of smell and taste.[2] At the same time, I was more than a little taken aback to discover much of the work of Monell was being supported by many of the fragrance suppliers in the industry. It appeared that they were quietly putting their collective

A treat to be with Dr. Morley Kare.

toes in the water to encourage Monell scientists in their search and study of how the sense of smell works—how odors affect our behavior and influence how we experience taste.

Beginning in 1982, the fund established industry and scientific advisory committees to review research grant proposals and advise us on scientific matters. Together, we agreed to support clinical specialists in universities and hospitals from New York to Canada to Tel Aviv, whose research resulted in a wide variety of studies.[3] More than fifty research grants and fellowships totaling over $1.4 million were made to research scientists in the fields of developmental, perceptual, social, and cognitive psychology, anthropology, biology, neuroscience, and related disciplines.

At the time, I was the first person outside the scientific community to establish a line of communication to neuroscientists and sensory psychologists. They unofficially credited the fund (and me) with bringing their work "out of the closet."

One of the doctors who most influenced and helped me build the fund into a truly respected and effective entity was Dr. Susan Schiffman. An energetic, vivacious, and innovative talent, she spent endless months with me as we worked to craft an organization that would be recognized globally for its expertise and innovation.

A specialist in many areas, including the development of techniques to employ the sense of smell to aid weight control, Dr. Schiffman was also a lead researcher in exploring the risk of a diminishing sense of smell in older people. I remember one test she conducted at a luncheon meeting we held at the Plaza Hotel in New York City. She invited waiters of various ages to the stage. They were blindfolded and fed applesauce. Those who were over sixty were unable to identify what they were tasting. It was one more unofficial affirmation of her studies that many people lose their ability to smell and taste as they age. This, she surmised, was the reason why the elderly lose interest in eating. By heightening smell experiences, Dr. Schiffman found this condition could be reversed to an amazing degree through stronger scent/taste impressions.

Sensory Revelations

Information was building that was destined to change a lot of preconceived notions in the industry, media, and certainly the lay public:

- Only the olfactory system puts the brain outside the body (courtesy of our noses) where, through the sense of smell, a wide range of emotional messages are delivered to the brain.
- The sense of smell (the old brain) is located in the limbic system where memory, creativity, emotions, and sexuality all reside. Contrary to popular opinion, the research also revealed we recall scent memories longer than those we experience visually.
- Brain mapping has revealed that, despite long-held beliefs, both sides of the brain light up depending on the introduction of different odors. Previously, scientists were under the impression that only the right side of the brain responded to odors.
- When we smell, we think.
- You can never have a relationship with someone whose smell you don't like (see chapter I, Dr. Margaret Mead).
- If you can't smell, you can't taste.
- Clues are being explored by the medical profession about the possibility that olfaction may hold links to the diagnosis of a number of diseases, including Alzheimer's. (Since smell and memory are so intricately connected, I was beginning to wonder myself if the

sense of smell could be employed to help those suffering from this dreadful disease. I spoke to several neuroscientists at Monell about it and was advised there was an ongoing investigation of possible connections.)

- In the case of our four other senses, we can block hearing, prevent seeing by closing our eyes, stop tasting at will, and withhold touching. Only the sense of smell continues to perform whether we like it or not as long as we are alive.
- Life begins with the first breath. Death, the last.

Successful Experiment

One of the most unexpected and surprising needs for our help came from the highly respected medical facility in New York City, Memorial Sloan Kettering Cancer Center. Drs. William Redd and Sharon Manne called to discuss a problem they were having with patients who panic during magnetic residence imaging (MRI) examinations. The problem resulted in the doctors having to abort the tests before they were completed.

After conferring with our scientific partners, the doctors received a research grant so they could pursue their investigation. Next, they met with perfumer members of the Fragrance Foundation who proposed that the smell of vanilla might prove calming. A Rube Goldberg–type contraption was built and placed near the MRI that released computer-timed puffs of the fragrance through two tubes that came to rest under the patient's nostrils. The doctors reported a positive response by an increasing number of patients who were willing to remain inside the MRI cylinder until the doctors had all the results they needed.

In the eighties, I was contacted by an executive from one of Japan's leading construction companies, Shimizu. The company was inquiring about the work we were doing and wanted to explore how it might help them. They were experiencing a major problem on their production line. Boredom and lack of interest by the workers were causing increasing accidents. We again put the company in touch with our sensory scientists, and as an experiment, they suggested releasing metered puffs of peppermint throughout the factory area. After working out the details of the fragrance and the necessary delivery system, the test went forward. Management reported an almost immediate change in attitude. Workers felt alert and attentive. Accidents went down; production went up. It was critical turnaround for the company and encouraged us to double our efforts.

Aroma-chology Arrives

In the early eighties, I coined (and we registered) the name Aroma-chology.[4] The purpose behind the name was to encourage the industry, which had long been introducing products in the aromatherapy field, to begin to reassess the science of the "interrelationship of psychology and the latest in fragrance technology." It had become clear from the research that it was possible to transmit a variety of specific feelings— relaxation, exhilaration, sensuality, happiness, and a sense of achievement—through odors. Four years later, the Fragrance Foundation sponsored a symposium to benefit the Olfactory Research Fund. Four authorities analyzed the impact Aroma-chology research could have on the global fragrance market in ten years.

Michael Sweeney, vice president of sales and marketing at International Flavors & Fragrances, suggested that "several factors make the time right for Aroma-chology to blossom throughout the world":

> First, today's conditions are creating a greater need for relief from pressures of daily life. Shelves are flooded with thousands of new products. Secondly, traditional methods of treating, healing and reducing stress are increasingly failing us. Europeans, who have long recognized the effects of herbal medicine, have a greater understanding and appreciation of essential oils and their usefulness. In France, aromatherapy is so common that it is covered by most insurance companies.
>
> Global marketers, if they want to enter this field, need to be aware of the differences (between aromatherapy and Aroma-chology) and need to be able to measure the accuracy of their claims.

Anthony J. Leardi reported on the historical importance of bathing in the Far East:

> Consumer product marketers have designed products to enhance the fragrant beauty of the bath. Moreover, they have incorporated Aroma-chology claims to provide additional mood enhancing benefits.

The desire to bring the beauty of the outdoors to our daily lives is, perhaps, most clearly exemplified by the continuing installation of fragrancing systems in some of the largest office buildings in the Far East. Aroma-chology fragrances introduced in the workplace can not only encourage productivity, but can bring the benefits of the refreshing outdoors to the daily grind.

People the world over are searching for ways to cope with many hectic and stressful demands of the modern day life. This is especially true in the Far East. Look at workers in Japan who are concerned with *karoshi*—literally, "too much work causes death."

Hans-Otto Schmidt focused on Medieval Europe:

Medicinal and herbaceous plants were frequently cultivated in monastic herb gardens and the herbs were used to restore health and to tickle the palate.

Taking comfort and pleasure from fragrant plant materials was something Medieval Europe learned from the Islamic culture, where doctors and scientist had a deeper understanding, not only for hygiene and medicine but also for the more refined pleasures of the senses.

Susan Babinsky defined the 1993 market from a US perspective:

Aroma-chology primary products:

- Traditional home fragrances
- Fragrances—men's and women's
- Selected specific toiletries: bath, hair, skin care
- Aroma-chology is the primary and key benefit communicated by the brands
- Total market size: $4.0 billion
- Primary products: traditional home fragrance
- Market size: $500 million
- Primary products: fragrances
- Market size: $3.3 billion

Despite the positive projections enhanced by the fund's scientific validations that certain types of fragrance ingredients had the ability to improve mood and enhance the quality of life, it was a hard—and eventually impossible—sell. The industry was in lockstep with the long-established aromatherapy product category. Period! Interestingly enough, in the years that followed, several entrepreneurial companies embraced the concept of Aroma-chology, and it even became a brand name for a variety of products.

Name-Droppers

In 1984, the board of the fund voted to change the name to Fragrance Research Fund to eliminate any confusion with the Fragrance Foundation. Eight years later, the name of the organization morphed into the Olfactory Research Fund, which had a short life because the public at large and the media were too unfamiliar with the word *olfactory* and often mistook it for "old factory." The board finally settled on renaming the organization the Sense of Smell Institute. It gained immediate acceptance by the public, the media, and the industry. Putting the name aside, the organization was about to face a problem it had not anticipated—a sudden lack of financial support.

What happened—after years of contributions that had allowed us to provide grants to those doctors who were studying a wide range of sensory opportunities to improve well-being—was hard to pin down. The most obvious and ominous was the blow of 9/11, which changed the world as we knew it. Nonprofits throughout the country quickly had to face a new reality: The tragedy forced a struggle for survival as support dried up. One of the more subliminal reasons was industry related. Several key supplier members had moved ahead on their own to support many of the doctors we were funding, but with exclusive rights to their work. Companies began to lock in the results of the scientific studies for proprietary purposes. Contributions to the Sense of Smell Institute slowly disappeared. It forced us to refocus our efforts on fund-raising and educational activities.

Fund-raising Fundamentals

It was always part of my responsibility to raise money, primarily within the industry, so that we would be self-sufficient and in a position to continue to award grants to groundbreaking sensory psychologists and neuropathologists in leading universities and hospitals around the world.

Left to right, Marvin Traub, President of Bloomingdale's, me, Dr. Lewis Thomas, noted neuropathologist and Dr. Fernando Aleu, President of the Sense of Smell Institute.

We established special events for the fragrance industry that included the presentation of the first annual Sense of Smell Awards in 1984. Thanks to Dr. Aleu's friendship with the noted neuropathologist Dr. Lewis Thomas, we were privileged to present him with the award. The retailing genius Marvin Traub, chairman of Bloomingdale's, was also a recipient. Ceremonies were held at the Waldorf Astoria. Dr. Thomas, author of the acclaimed book *Lives of the Cell*, noted in his acceptance remarks, "If I were a young researcher interested in making a career in science and in neurobiology, I would want to learn something important about the human brain. I would look around for a field about which nobody now knows much of anything and be ready, as all good researchers must be, to gamble. By picking the mysteries of olfaction, I would count on a professional lifetime of one surprise after another."

Trolling for Dollars

From 1985 to 1994, we presented Tiffany Medals of Honor on stage at the annual Fragrance Foundation FiFi Awards. The medals were embedded in a sleek ebony base that accommodated an abstract crystal design by Pierre

Dinand (the designer of the FiFi), interpreting the spirit of fragrance wafting in the air. In 1988, Dr. Jack Mausner was elected president of the board of the fund. Under his direction, we developed awards presentations in three categories: gold vermeil, sterling silver, and bronze, each of which represented five-year pledges totaling $100,000, $50,000, and $25,000, respectively. Quest International, a major industry supplier, was the first contributor of $100,000. Presenting the awards each year was an ideal opportunity to expose the accomplishments of the fund to the many hundreds of members of the international fragrance community who attended the FiFi ceremonies. In acknowledging the contribution of Quest, Dr. Mausner encouraged other members of the industry to pledge their support to fund significant research related to the sense of smell and the psychological benefits of fragrance. The following year, Scent Seal (producer of magazine inserts, eventually purchased by Arcade) also donated $100,000. Many other companies followed suit with varying amounts.

Funding the Future

In 1992, the Scientific Sense of Smell Award was presented at a gala dinner to fund grant recipients Drs. Richard Axel (investigator, Howard Hughes Medical Institute at Columbia University) and Linda Buck (assistant professor at Harvard University). A few years later, the ingenious honorees would be awarded the Nobel Prize in recognition of their revolutionary discovery of a large family of smell genes. Buck and Axel found that each of the different genes respond to a small group of odors, and together, these sensory genes were able to recognize the thousands of scents that mammals can smell. With this discovery, scientists can now ask and research essential questions about how odors are detected and how the brain can interpret these signals.

To report all the activities of the organization, at the suggestion of Dr. Cain, we began to publish a slick newsletter, the *Olfactory Review*, which several years later became the *Aroma-chology Review* to more closely reflect the changing work of the renamed Sense of Smell Institute. It carried news of research being carried on around the world, scientific book reviews, and articles by scientists we had funded. The *Review* was distributed to supporters of the institute, as well as members of academia, media, and the fragrance industry.

Enid Nemy, New York Times reporter with Geoffrey Beene, fashion designer.

In 1995, we published a compendium of olfactory research that was a "first" to document the twelve years of research results (1982–1994) supported by the institute. Edited by Dr. Avery Gilbert, the compendium included a timeline tracing the history of the founding of the Sense of Smell Institute and detailed the research results of the twenty-seven neuroscientists the institute had supported over the years. Dr. Gilbert also provided an introduction to each section in the book "in order to place the reports into a larger context for the reader." The compendium included a fascinating chapter contributed by Anthony Synnott of the Department of Sociology and Anthropology at Concordia University, Montreal, Canada,[5] featuring famous poets and members of the medical, academic, and scientific communities entitled "Roses, Coffee, and Lovers: The Meanings of Smell."

The institute was always dedicated to spearheading new fund-raising awards programs. In November 1994, the board decided to consolidate all its awards presentations under the banner of one major annual fund-raising event, the Night of Honors. It took place in the delegates' dining room at the United Nations and commemorated over a decade of programs supported by the institute, as well as its educational and public outreach activities. At the ceremonies, the Richard B. Solomon Award was introduced and honored Diane Ackerman, who had authored the prize-winning book *A Natural History of Senses*, which WETA public-service television produced as a miniseries. The award was presented annually to an individual, school, member of the media, or museum (including science centers) for unique contributions in creating public awareness of the sense of smell and human response to odors. As a matter of fact, I was the happy recipient with my co-author, Linda Dyett, for our book, *The Secrets of Aromatic Jewelry*, published in France by Flammarion.

Visualizing Smell

The same year, we registered the service mark "Get in Touch with Your Sense of Smell," which received approval by the US Patent & Trademark Office. It became the basis of a public-service advertising campaign launched in the *New York Times* and also appeared in publications of many of the magazine members of the Fragrance Foundation. The graphics for the four-color campaign featured a photograph of an original oil painting of a full-blown red rose (pictured inside an elegant gold frame) by French artist Guy Begin. Body copy for the ad read "The deepest emotional response to a rose comes from its aroma, which no artist can capture in even the most exquisite painting or photograph. And it is not just the fragrance of flowers that influences and motivates us. The positive impact of the wonderful world of smells and odors affects our feelings of well-being. A particular scent can make a person confident and productive while another can reduce stress and have a relaxing effect. Leading a full, happy life means understanding the importance of all your senses." The tagline: "Get in touch with your sense of smell and enjoy the pleasures it gives you." Designed by a talented graphic artist, Julia Ptasznik, the ad was headlined "Without the scent, it's just a pretty picture."

Readers were invited to send us self-addressed, stamped envelopes to receive more information about their sense of smell. The response was immediate and enthusiastic. Each respondent was sent a series of informative pamphlets we had prepared that offered easy reading about the important differences between Aroma-chology and aromatherapy, basic details about how we smell, the history and anthropology of smell, and techniques and exercises to improve the sense of smell. All carried the tagline "Get in Touch with Your Sense of Smell."

Youthful Scent-sations

We developed the first annual National Sense of Smell Day in 1994, which was launched and celebrated with olfactory displays and interactive exhibitions in science centers and museums in thirteen cities. Special events and activities entertained and educated visitors of all ages about the sense of smell, human reactions to odors, and the positive effects of fragrance. There were treasure hunts, using odors as clues, preschool scratch-and-sniff storytelling, plant and herb displays to touch and smell, and animal demonstrations to reveal how different species use their sense of smell. Arts and craft sessions provided adults and children an opportunity to make potpourri and spice sachets. Among the most popular activities were various odor IQ tests. Participants identified a variety of popular aromas to test their smell acuity.

The event was so successful that National Sense of Smell Day became an annual happening for over ten years. When funding was no longer available, several science centers and museums continued participation on their own every April.

In the eight years before the Sense of Smell Institute was dissolved, one of my colleagues who had worked with me during the years of the institute's growth, Theresa Molnar, undertook the responsibility of building career guidance fairs for students in high schools. They turned out to be extremely successful and received outstanding industry participation and support from a variety of companies, including Givaudan, Avon, *CosmoGirl* magazine, and Elizabeth Arden. The fair was held in the fall of each year, and approximately 125–150 students from schools throughout New York City attended. Teachers came to observe and gave the fairs an A+ for providing students with the experience of interacting with industry members and absorbing the ins and outs of various careers in the world of fragrance. One of the initial purposes of the fair was to demonstrate to students, especially girls, the importance of science and math to an industry that is considered merely glamorous to the outside world. They learned that the creation of perfume and cosmetics is dependent on skills associated with chemistry, as well as package engineering and design know-how. Schools are now emphasizing STEM studies, and it is gratifying to realize that SOSI was once again ahead of its time.

Despite the extraordinary success and global contributions of the Sense of Smell Institute, it was essentially abandoned after I retired. Dr. Avery Gilbert stepped down as board chair. Fortunately, Dr. Craig Warren, who at that time was associated with International Flavors & Fragrances, served on our scientific committee and made himself available to provide information and contacts in the olfactory community. Dr. Warren later became associated with the University of San Diego in its chemosensory research laboratory. He continued to help whenever the fund had the need.

I still believe the closing down of SOSI was a great loss for the fragrance industry, the research community, and the public at large. Yet I am consoled by the realization that the work of the institute helped to open up a global and media awareness of the importance of the sense of smell and, indeed, all of the senses.

The subject has become part of the fabric of brain research and resonates in medical, psychological, and educational circles, as well as in advertising and marketing across a wide swath of industries. As a matter of fact, one of the latest revelations in evaluating the importance of the sense of smell received coverage in the *Economist* magazine (October 2, 2014),[6] the *New York Times* blog (October 1, 2014),[7] and the *New York Times* newspaper (October 14, 2014).[8] Each revealed the possibility that the inability to smell was a clue to a shortened lifespan. Under the aegis of the University of Chicago, the study was conducted by Drs. Martha McClintock (who, years before, had received support for her work from our Sense of Smell Institute) and Jayant Pinto, who was quoted in the article in the *New York Times* as warning that "loss of the sense of smell should not be ignored. There are treatable causes of olfactory loss. So if people have problems, they should get evaluated. This is a gross indication of your health, so if you're having some trouble, you should see your doctor." Dr. McClintock, in explaining the results of the study to the *Economist*, stressed that "smell may be the canary in the coal mine of human health."

One of the most startling research revelations surfaced in the *New York Times* newspaper (October 14, 2014):

Over the last decade or so, scientists have discovered that odor receptors are not solely confined to the nose, but found throughout the body—the liver, the heart, the kidneys, and even sperm—where they play a pivotal role in a host of physiological functions.

Now, a team of biologists at Ruhr University Bochum in Germany has also found our skin is bristling with olfactory receptors. ... [The lead researcher, Dr. Hanns Hatt, has found] genetic evidence [that] suggests nearly every organ in the body contains olfactory receptors.

"I've been arguing for the importance of these receptors for years," said Dr. Hatt, who calls himself an ambassador of smell, and whose favorite aromas are basil, thyme and rosemary. "It was a hard fight."

But researchers have gradually awakened to the biological importance of these molecular sniffers and the promise they hold for the diagnosis and treatment of disease. ... No doubt, few scientists ever imagined that fragrance sold at perfume counters would possess any significant medical benefits.

How thrilling! If ever there was a moment to repeat the Fragrance Foundation's invitation to the public to "test their sense of smell," (see chapter XV) this is it. What an indispensable service that would be.

And I am particularly heartened by a feature story on the importance of the sense of smell to emotional well-being which appeared on the front page of the business section of the *New York Times* on March 15, 2015. It reviewed the work of Audrey Gruss, founder of the Hope for Depression Research Foundation, and her search for a fragrance that could be comforting to people with depression.

The olfactory system has definitely moved center stage in the scientific world's search for solutions to life's emotional challenges. Eureka!

---

1. Aristotle was the first to recognize the critical role of all the senses "in developing our humanity."
2. I was particularly impressed with Drs. Avery N. Gilbert, Charles J. Wysocki, and Pamela Dalton and their creative insights into the world of olfaction. When *National Geographic* magazine began its plans for a national smell survey, the editors turned to Gilbert and Wysocki. The doctors addressed the effects of aging on our smell acuity. The landmark survey ran in the September 1986 issue, and 1.42 million people responded. Working with Avery led me to recommend him to Givaudan when I learned the company was considering setting up a sensory center in its laboratories. The president, Alvin Lindsay,

eventually invited Dr. Gilbert to join the team to oversee their cutting-edge explorations of the sense of smell. As Dr. Gilbert became more involved with the industry, I turned to him to lend his talents to the Olfactory Research Fund as scientific affairs director. Later, he joined the board of trustees. When Dr. Jack Mausner stepped down as chairman of the board in 1999, I proposed Dr. Gilbert as his replacement to the nominating committee. He was unanimously elected by the board, and served until 2003.

3. "Aging and Odor" (Dr. Susan Shiffman, Duke Medical Center); "Behavior and Odor" (Dr. Howard Ehrlichman, Queens College); "Fragrance Use and Social Interaction" (Drs. Glenn Shean and John Nezek, College of William and Mary); "Congruent and Incongruent Odors; The Effect on Human Approach Behavior" (Dr. Susan C. Knasko, Monell Chemical Senses Center); "Roses, Coffee, and Lovers: The Meaning of Smell" (Dr. Anthony Synnott and his research partners, David Howes and Constance Classen, Concordia University, Montreal, Canada); "Memory and Odor" (Dr. Trygg Engen, Brown University); and "Sleep and Odor" (Dr. Peter Badia, Bowling Green State University).

4. After the first year, we dropped the registration mark so that "Aroma-chology" would be available in the public domain, making it easier for industry members to replace "aromatherapy" as the term to describe fragrances formulated to provide positive behavioral effects.

5. Dr. Synnott's partners in his research were David Howes and Constance Classen.

6. "Dr. McClintock and Pinto were prompted to conduct their investigation because they knew olfactory problems can forewarn of neurodegenerative disease such as Alzheimer's and Parkinson's. … Moreover, a good sense of smell helps keep people healthy by detecting pathogens and toxins in the air, stimulates appetite and aids memory, emotions, and intimacy. The researchers therefore had good reason to wonder if measuring smell loss might predict mortality. …

   "No one is suggesting not being able to smell leads directly to death. … They note that olfaction relies on a turnover of stem cells (from which other sorts of cells develop) to maintain its functioning. Not to be able to smell, they speculate, may signal more general inability to generate and renew" ("Longevity and the sense of smell," the *Economist*, October 2, 2014).

7. "[The study] controlled for many factors—age, sex, socioeconomic status, smoking, alcohol intake, education, body mass index, race, hypertension, diabetes, heart attack, emphysema, stroke and diet. But still, people who could not detect the odors [rose, lavender, orange, fish, and peppermint] were more than three times likely to die within five years than those who could. … The researchers believe that the decline in the ability to smell is an indicator of some other age-related degeneration, and is not itself a cause of death" (Nicholas Bakalar, "Failing Sense of Smell May Predict Sooner Death," *New York Times* blog, October 1, 2014).

8. " 'More than 15 olfactory receptors that exist in the nose are also found in the human skin cells,' said the lead researcher, Dr. Hanns Hatt. Not only that, but exposing one of these receptors (colorfully named OR2AT4) to a synthetic sandalwood odor known

as Sandalore sets off a cascade of molecular signals that appears to induce healing in injured tissue. ...

"The presence of scent receptors outside the nose may seem odd at first, but as Dr. Hatt and others have observed, odor receptors are among the most evolutionarily ancient chemical sensors in the body, capable of detecting a multitude of compounds, not solely those drifting through the air.

" 'If you think of olfactory receptors as specialized chemical detectors, instead of as receptors in your nose that detect smell, then it makes a lot of sense for them to be in other places,' said Jennifer Pluznick, an assistant professor of physiology at Johns Hopkins University, who in 2009 found that olfactory receptors help control metabolic function and regulate blood pressure in the kidneys of mice" (Alex Stone, "Smell Turns Up in Unexpected Places," *New York Times*, October 14, 2014).

XIII

Word Play

Smell is a potent wizard that transports us a thousand miles and all the years we have lived.

—Helen Keller

If you have ever been on a treasure hunt (and who hasn't?), you know how tinged the experience is with expectation and anticipation. In my case, I didn't even know what I was destined to discover. My search in the early eighties was focused on finding historical documents and memorabilia, as well as perfume historians who might provide a deeper understanding of the fragrance in people's lives throughout recorded time. It was all for the cause of our upcoming exhibition, *Scents of Time*, which was to open in New York at the Museum of the City of New York in 1987. Along the way, pictures, and articles began to surface, revealing stunning pieces of jewelry (rings, bracelets, necklaces, earrings, garment clips) that were designed specifically to hold perfume.

A year or so after the exhibition ended (see chapter IV), I became intrigued with the idea that this jewelry and its history had the makings of a fascinating book. An unexpected meeting with Suzanne Tise'Isore, the charming editorial director of the French art book publisher Flammarion, brought the dream into focus. She had visited my office in New York to inquire whether I could assist her in the preparation of a book on perfume bottles that Flammarion was planning to publish. I said, "Yes ... but," and I told her about the book I wanted to write. She agreed it could offer a new twist on the subject and wanted to know more.

Naturally, Suzanne was interested in seeing the materials I had collected over a ten-year period. The depth and breadth of *objets d'art* I shared with her sealed the deal. She was certain we could also secure additional pieces and photographs from museums and private collectors around the world. She believed, as I did, that this could be a book that would be the first of its kind to present a unique and largely unexplored decorative art form within the historical context of fashion, fragrance, and social trends.

I invited a talented writer and researcher I was already working with, Linda Dyett, to join the project in 1982 to assist in a worldwide search for historical and modern pieces. Linda, a journalist in her own right, became my collaborator and coauthor.

A beautifully illustrated full-color eight-by-ten book was published in 1998. It artfully traces the history (ancient and modern) of jewelry designs that held scent. One hundred ninety-two lushly laid-out pages include 150 color plates and revealing quotes from famous artists and poets, including Picasso.[1]

Linda and I appeared together at the book-signing launch party held at Bergdorf Goodman in New York. The store also created a mini exhibition of pieces featured in the book. Shoppers enthusiastically bought the book, which we were more than happy to autograph. For the record, I have been told *Secrets of Aromatic Jewelry* is still available on Amazon at ever-increasing prices.

Writing Matters

In the years before writing *Secrets*, I conceived a quarterly publication, *Fragrance Forum*, to provide the industry with in-depth information not only about what the Fragrance Foundation was doing but about societal and scientific changes that could influence the future of fragrance usage. To kick off the launch issue in the summer of 1984, Dr. Fernando Aleu, president of the Fragrance Foundation, wrote in a front-page editorial:

> The paper you are holding in your hands represents a new effort of the Fragrance Foundation: *Fragrance Forum*. It will be a quarterly publication which today sees the light for the first time.
>
> Many subjects will be addressed, too, but coverage will not be based on their potential news value. This is not a newspaper. Each will be considered for their significance not only from marketing, retailing, and advertising points of view, but also financial, scientific, and managerial perspectives. The world of data processing and cybernetics will be explored. These contents will be handled not only with the perspective gained from the past but also with the speculation of what the future is likely to bring.

Perfume Aficionado

In the first year of publication, *Fragrance Forum* carried an insightful interview with fashion's grande dame Diana Vreeland. Her genius had energized and inspired the world of high fashion for over a half a century both in her role as fashion editor for *Harper's Bazaar* for twenty-eight years and editor in chief for *Vogue* for ten. When I spoke with her, she was a special consultant at the Costume Institute at the Metropolitan Museum of Art. We met in her dramatic red-lacquered living room to talk about her passion for fragrance. What fun that was. She definitely liked to be provocative. "People have to realize they have to put on a lot of fragrance if it's going to have any impact at all. Just a dab doesn't mean a thing. I need flowers everywhere and lots of gorgeous fragrances to create unforgettable impressions, exciting moods. Fragrance, like allure, is an aura around you. You can't go out and order it. It is something you personally project; it's a part of you. The memory of fragrance is irresistible."

When I asked her if fragrance ads were a part of that allure, she answered, "No! I don't think fragrance ads are flirtatious enough. If I were bringing out a new fragrance, I would pull out all the plugs when it comes to advertising. It would be everywhere. Everybody would hear about it. I think the industry is more into the techniques of advertising than expressing the message of the fragrances themselves. But with good advertising or bad, I have always found that a great scent is always sought out and found. So I say, take advantage of everything beautiful, exciting, heroic, including fragrance, so that life is never boring—neither are you."

Infamous for her dedication to scents that make a statement, who could doubt Mrs. Vreeland's reaction to the news in the fall of 2014 that her grandson, Alexander Vreeland, had launched a Diana Vreeland five-scent collection? A year later, he added two provocative perfumes, Smashingly Brilliant and Daringly Different.

In addition to interviews with famous fashionistas, each issue of the *Fragrance Forum* featured trendsetters from a variety of fields writing about their areas of expertise. Subjects as broad-based as the influence of weather events on fragrance perceptions to emerging ethnic and teen markets written by experts in their fields filled our pages. We eventually included a quarterly portfolio of "Great Launches" to spotlight new fragrances that had made an impact on the market.

The POW of Personalities

In the fall of 1994, I started a front-page series, "In Conversation With …," which became an industry favorite. My first interview was with Yves Saint Laurent. We met in his suite at the Pierre Hotel. He was in New York to launch his new fragrance, Champagne. It was Yves Saint Laurent's introduction in 1997 of Opium perfume, however, that caused a sensation and an international controversy. I remember a public demonstration in front of the Park Avenue building in Manhattan that housed the headquarters of Squibb (the US licensee of the YSL Perfume Company) decrying the name, which many considered too positive a reference to a harmful drug. Nevertheless, the consumers were titillated by the concept, and in short order, Opium perfume was a major hit around the world.

For me, the launch party for Opium aboard the hundred-plus-year-old tall sailing ship, *Peking*, was an industry tour de force. The ship was moored at the South Street Seaport in lower Manhattan. (Still is!) I was lucky enough to be invited to drop by early in the afternoon to watch the ship being prepared for the party. What an experience! A thousand-pound golden Buddha was hoisted aboard and placed center stage on the deck. Tall bamboo poles were arranged throughout, entwined with white cattleya orchids, as was the Buddha. Banners of purple, red, and gold fluttered in the wind.

When I returned in the evening, the deck itself was strewn with orchid petals. A crowd of celebrities, fragrance industry types, and media representatives, plus YSL himself, had joined the celebration.

A memorable visit with Yves Saint Laurent.

Anyone who was there will never forget the magical moment when a full moon rose over the Brooklyn Bridge and a raft-like barge floated toward the *Peking*. It was a mesmerizing sight made even more so as special strobe lights revealed "YSL" spelled out in gigantic floral letters. Almost instantaneously, a barrage of fireworks lit up the night sky. It was a catch-your-breath moment, and I can honestly say I don't believe there has ever been another fragrance launch that created such a sensation.

At the beginning of the interview, Yves spoke to me in French through an interpreter. Slowly, however, he warmed to our conversation and began to share his views in English. He spoke of the changing roles of women and the implications for fragrance and fashion.

Women in the nineties are open about their sexuality. So are the perfumes they wear. I design my fragrance and fashions with this very much in mind. Women, especially working women, are taking more and more power. I believe they expect their perfumes to give inner strength and energy. Everything I see, hear, or touch inspires me. I haven't been in New York for eleven years. Now that I am back, I wonder why I stayed away so long. I am so excited by the energy of the city. The sexuality I feel in the street by both men and women. When I design my next collection, I will devote myself to capturing New York's energy. It doesn't exist anywhere else. For me, perfume must be adapted to fashion, not the other way around. Fashion leads the way, perfume follows. For both, I am influenced by the seasons, winter/summer, as well as a woman's many moods. Fragrance is so important in today's world because fashion is everywhere. It is the grand star in everyone's life, available to all women wherever they live, whatever they do.

My interview with Carolina Herrera revealed her fragrance adventures actually began when I invited her to be a FiFi Awards presenter at the ceremonies held at Avery Fisher Hall, Lincoln Center, in 1985. During the reception, she had the opportunity to talk with Dr. Fernando Aleu, and their conversation didn't stop there. Just a few years later, Compar introduced Ms. Herrera's first namesake fragrance, which has become one of our industry's success stories. When I spoke with Carolina Herrera in her wonderfully comfortable living-room-like office (*Fragrance Forum*, Fall 1996) she shared two fascinating facts about her teenage yearnings:

> I wanted to be a vamp, like Marlene Dietrich, and thought it would be wonderful to wear slinky black gowns, silky seamed stockings, lots of plumes, and heavy perfumes.
>
> Diana Vreeland was my mentor and inspiration. She literally pushed me into a career of designing. I discovered in fashion, and now in fragrance, women aspire to beautiful fantasies. Everything we wear must suit its time. Reality can be virtual. The social context in which fashion and fragrance are born create new dynamics. Fashions and fragrances must complement each other, and today's consumer knows that very well. When I look at the great classic fragrances, I do admire them and realize that they transcend time and are constantly contemporary. That is always my goal, to create timeless fashions and timeless fragrances. The one thing I believe about fragrance with all my heart is that a woman or a man, for that matter, should really wear it. Subtlety is not what wearing fragrance is all about. Just as fashion is a fulfilling experience for the eye, fragrance must be the same for the nose.

Donna Karan and her husband, the late sculptor Stephan Weiss, joined me for breakfast at the Royalton Hotel in New York (*Fragrance Forum*, Fall 1994). The common denominator that we all shared was the importance of self-discovery through the senses. Donna mused:

> When I walked into the fragrance project, I was a little skeptical, even cynical. Now, fragrance has become a fashion for me. It means more to me than ever before. The project has expanded the wonderful relationship I have with my husband in a magnificent new way. It has given us another dimension of expression. Designers in today's world are setting the standards. Don't forget, people wear the designers, wear the fragrance, buy into the fantasy. As far as my designs are concerned, I believe the consumer knows what I stand for. But it's not about clothing, it's about a lifestyle. I want what I design, whether it's fashion or fragrance, to become a classic. I look at it. I wear it. I treasure

it. My designs are about warmth, touch, comfort, sophistication, and sexuality.

Karl Lagerfeld sent me his stream of consciousness observations (*Fragrance Forum*, Fall 1998) about the contemporary fragrance, fashion, and social scene:

> Fashions, fragrances, and photographs are three things that for me are totally connected. Photography of the twenties, for instance, represents the culture and fashion of the time—even if it was not intended to be "fashion" in the beginning. And this is true of fragrances, too. Often people realize that reality only much later, or they think that fashion and fragrances are not part of our culture. They are! I am a fashion freak and always had been, I love fragrances, use them, like to smell them on others. Life would be horrible without fragrance.

Oscar de la Renta (*Fragrance Forum*, Fall 1999) invited me to visit him in his elegant stark-white offices many weeks before the rave reviews broke in Paris about his fall collection and his being chosen to design Mrs. Clinton's inaugural wardrobe:

> Fashions change and with rare exceptions are forgotten by the public. But the classic fragrances, like an invisible dress, endure. Fragrances are always being discovered by a new generation, and the designer's name is kept alive. The one thing that makes fashion and fragrance especially exciting is that the world is getting smaller and smaller. The woman today is international. There are no classifications. You no longer recognize the nationality of the woman by the way she is dressed. Lifestyle is what counts: what a woman wants to wear, what her interests are, where she likes to go, and how she lives and not where.

During one of my trips to Paris, I met Chanel's renown perfumer, Jacques Polge (*Fragrance Forum*, Spring 1995), in the historic and romantic apartment of Mlle Chanel on the Rue Cambon. There, amid the glamorous memorabilia and mementos that reflect the life and times of this awesome and influential woman, we talked of the wonders of Mlle Chanel and her trailblazing breakthrough fragrance, Chanel No. 5:

> What I like about fragrance is the poetic element, the fact that fragrance is a silent language that does not use words. One can express with fragrance things that cannot be expressed in any other way. It is the very subjective, invisible, silent part of fragrance which greatly appeals to me. A moment was coming that the perception of perfume, which for such a long time was only considered from the point of view of seduction, was changing and now many men and women cannot start their day without fragrance; and that probably means all the psychological elements are important. The key, I believe, is that fragrance makes people feel good about themselves.

In 1969, the Fashion Group published a book titled *Your Future in the Beauty Business by 17 Famous Members of the Fashion Group Inc.* A group of executive women (including me) were each asked to write a chapter designed to help future employees discover opportunities available to them in each of our respective fields. My subject, of course, was the fragrance industry. I titled it "The Field of Fragrance: The Dollars (and Other Rewards) of Scents." One of the pieces of advice I gave is still applicable today: "Finally, may I say that in the fragrance industry, a youthful approach is today a tremendous asset. It is sought after by all companies because it personifies the mood and tempo of contemporary consumers of all ages. It also offers the company the type of vitality and creative thinking that can move merchandise."

Thirty-six years later, the editorial board of Scribner's contacted me regarding contributing a chapter to a three-volume set they were planning to publish, *Encyclopedia of Clothing and Fashion.* The editor in chief was a colleague and friend, Valerie Steele, the extraordinary curator of the museum at the Fashion Institute of Technology. I was delighted to be asked. My contribution, "Perfume: In and Out of Fashion," fell into the general category of body adornments (makeup, masks, and tattoos). I traced the history of fragrance from the early Egyptians to France and its royal courts. Included were details about the emergence of Gabrielle Chanel in the twentieth century and her influence on fashion designers that followed in her footsteps. I made special note that the important link between fashion and fragrance really took hold after World War II and certainly was the beginning of what would become the global realization of both. My closing paragraph turned out to be quite prescient:

> The future promises to embrace designer-inspired fragrances for the home, public spaces, outer-space stations, and space capsules. The sense of smell has never before in history been so brilliantly redesigned to join an olfactory adventure which absolutely knows no bounds.

In the late seventies, while on a trip to Paris, I visited the Centre Pompidou, which was devoting a major exhibition to the *Forgotten Ear*. As I remember, a monumental ear was the centerpiece of the exhibition. Visitors could enter it and experience for themselves the miracle of hearing. Like everyone else, I was impressed, but as far as I was concerned, ignorance about hearing didn't hold a candle to how little was known about our noses and the sense of smell (see chapter XII).

Inspired by the Paris exhibition, when I returned to New York, I worked on a paperback titled *The Forgotten Nose*. One of its chapters, "Past Sense," covered a variety of early revelations revealing previously unpublished facts about when, why, and how the sense of smell evolved and the importance of noses to each of us, physically and psychologically. Since the source of the smelling experience still occupies the same portion of the brain as it did from the very beginning of time, it is considered the most primitive of our senses. The book also focused on the science of smell and how our sensory decisions are made based on smell. We gathered fun facts and foibles, tracing human attitudes and prejudices about noses and included notes, quotes, and anecdotes of famous poets and writers through history. The poet Rudyard Kipling proclaimed:

> "Smells are surer than sounds or sights
> to make your heart-strings crack."

The Forgotten Nose became a staple in the foundation's library[2] and a favorite of the industry, students, and the public.

I also wrote the introduction to a charming book, *NOSEtalgia—The Smells That Take You Back*. It was published by Andrews McMeel Publishing in 2005. Conceived and written by Michael Gitter, vice president of Max Costume Media LLC (who holds the trademark), with Sylvie Vaccari and Carol Bobolts, the book was a madcap, whimsically illustrated romp through the world of smells from coffee to baseballs, peanut butter, plastic toys, shampoos, automobiles, popcorn, and naturally, fragrance. Ten scratch-and-sniff scents provided by a specialist in the fragrance industry, Arcade Marketing, were scattered throughout as an extra bit of fun. I was particularly enthusiastic about Vicks VapoRub because of its role as one of the first meaningful modern products designed for its aromatic benefits. Still does the job, as anyone with a clogged nose will attest.

The publications we prepared for the consumer covered every conceivable topic on the subject of scent: The History, the Mystery, the Enjoyment of Fragrance; The Male Fragrance Adventure; Beauty and the Bath; and Guide to Collecting Perfume Bottles.

We often worked closely with the *New York Times* to create leaflets that were inserted into the paper, particularly during Fragrance Week. One that caused quite a stir was *The Fragrance Lover's Guide*. It lauded fragrances as near-magic potions that not only excite and exhilarate, but subliminally power sexual attraction.

One of our most successful efforts for the industry was the annual publication of the *Reference Guide*. A paperback, it featured every company in the industry, whether they were Fragrance Foundation members or not, and listed all the fragrances each marketed, including descriptions of the ingredients, as well as the years of introduction. The guide became an industry bible that was referred to in offices and on the road. After I retired, it became a shadow of its former self and was eventually abandoned for a lightweight version. Today, it is just another Fragrance Foundation memory.

---

1. Few companies in the industry were inspired to introduce decorative jewelry that held fragrance except for specialty gifts at holiday time. In 2014, the designer Kilan Hennesey announced in Paris that "perfume is an accessory, the same as shoes and handbags are. But it is invisible." His solution was to create a collection of necklaces

and scented bracelets (for men and women). His future plans included rings and earrings to hold fragrance.

2. The New York Public Library lauded the foundation's extraordinary collection of books, videos, and publications as one of the most complete on the subject of fragrance in the world.

XIV

Moving Up

The only place success comes before work is in the dictionary.
—Vince Lombardi

W hen I moved the Fragrance Foundation and Annette Green Associates to a carriage house on East Thirtieth Street in New York in the late eighties, there was no doubt we had entered a bright new future. The Fragrance Foundation was on its way to unprecedented heights of success and was now able to increasingly support staffing and membership activities, as well as the move.

A two-story eight-hundred-square-foot treasure, the house sat serenely (and secretly) behind a New Orleans–style town house (painted yellow), owned and lived in by of one of *Gourmet* magazine's superb travel and food editors, Geri Trotta. Inside, a Tiffany glass window, visible from the front door, was surrounded by walls finished in raw dark-brown wood. Upstairs, a soaring thirty-foot sloping skylight covered a wide-open space that included a small kitchen. Under the skylight, a wall of folding, windowed doors was ready to be unlocked at the first sign of spring. They opened to overlook a charming, colorful, and fragrant garden.

The house was reachable from the street through its own black double-door entry. A wide pathway led to the carriage house. It began life in the eighteen hundreds to protect the horse and carriage of a doctor who lived with his family in the "main" house on the street. After the Second World War, Geri Trotta and her husband, Mark Shaw, a noted fashion photographer, bought the property, and the carriage house became his

studio. Models were a constant presence, and a room was set aside on the first floor for them to change their clothes and apply makeup. A wall of mirrors was a glamorous reminder of the purpose of the room for several members of my staff who settled in with typewriters, file cabinets, and telephones.

Nearby, a large room, complete with a real fireplace, became our library and conference center. We created an office and file room in a space at the entrance of the house to serve as the domain of our major domo, Ina Gray. We placed a very large ficus tree in the center of the room on the second floor where it flourished under that incredible skylight (which I have to admit leaked when it rained or snowed). Visitors were invited to gather in a living-room-like setting. Bookcases lined one wall, and we hung dramatic photographs of flowers and fragrance posters throughout the space. My desk and workplace were set up beneath the skylight. Across the room, the foundation's talented director, Mary Ellen Lapsansky, and my partner, Lois Berk, had their workstations. The environment was so congenial, Lois and I considered it our home away from home and spent hours at night and over the weekends on projects

that demanded our constant attention as they moved toward immutable deadlines.

Geri Trotta was a charming and generous landlady and lent a fascinating literary bent to our stay. The carriage house itself was a favorite of the industry and inspired creativity. Some of our most exciting and original projects were born in that enchanting environment. When spring came, we pushed open the folding doors and found ourselves in what felt like our own tree house, welcoming birds flying in and out.

Ten years later we left, reluctantly. We had outgrown the space. Our next move was two blocks up to Thirty-Second Street to a lovely art deco building. We rented the entire fourteenth floor, which, happily, included a long wall of windows. The natural light was spectacular. The decorator created a green-and-white garden motif and filled the space with lots of plants. All the office dividers were lattice work, and white lacquer garden furniture set the mood in the reception area. The obvious goal was to help make the transition from the carriage house bearable.

The Town House Capers

In the mid-nineties, the foundation had reached a new plateau, and the board's plans for the future coalesced around the creation of America's first fragrance museum. Where it would be housed was the question, which brings me to the tale of the town house that got away. A decision was made to pursue the possibility of buying a property on the east side of Manhattan. It was certainly the right moment. Real estate prices were down, and inventory was high. With the help of an agent, Mary Ellen and I began the search. What a wide range of town houses we visited, from residences with French doors leading to exquisitely planted gardens to houses with soaring freestanding glass staircases. Several buildings were fully equipped as offices, including wiring for all necessary technology. One we visited was a six-story town house located in the mid-fifties between Lexington and Third Avenues. It was perfectly laid out to allow our new museum to inhabit the first and second floors, with offices above. There was also a finished basement for storage and office equipment.

The board joined me in seeing the house on several occasions and agreed, if it passed inspection, that it would be perfect for the Fragrance Foundation. It was particularly well-located near most of our member companies, and it was a heavy foot-traffic area, which would certainly benefit the museum. From a practical standpoint, we discovered there was a local freelance superintendent available who serviced many of the houses on the block. At that time, the town house was on the market for $1.5 million. Because of the enthusiasm of the board, I met with representatives of the city to determine what advantages we would have as a nonprofit foundation incorporating a museum. They were extremely positive about the possibility and indicated there would be tax breaks and many other advantages for such an operation. The museum was the raison d'être. After a series of meetings, a number of documents were drawn up for our attorney to review. We were well on our way, and there seemed to be no roadblocks.

At the eleventh hour, however, board president Jeanette Wagner became fearful about the ability of our all-female staff to deal with maintaining the house. The long and short of it, despite our assurances that we had access to a superintendent who would care for the building, was that the board decided not to go forward. Instead, we moved to the tenth and eleventh floors in the building we were already in. The eleventh floor was to be devoted to the perfume museum. In fact, it was from one of the eleventh-floor windows that we sadly viewed the tragic disappearance of the Twin Towers on 9/11.

XV

Scent-ertainment

Favorite Co-conspirators

Alvin "Bud" Lindsay, president of Givaudan-Roure and treasurer of the foundation

Herb Rickman, deputy for the fashion industries in New York, office of Mayor Koch

Georges Gotlib, perfume bottle and package designer

We never do anything well, unless we love it for its own sake.
— Mary Wollstonecraft

In the early eighties, the steps of the grand plaza leading to the famed New York Public Library on Fifth Avenue and Forty-Second Street became a glamorous outdoor stage during the week of the FiFi Awards ceremonies. It was part of our long-term plans to foster interest in the pleasures of all the senses to the public at large. For five years, each spring we presented sensory, fun-filled events as part of the kickoff for what we titled "Fragrance Week in New York." To set the mood, we commissioned the Gramercy Park Flower Shop to create huge multi-floral wreaths to hang around the necks of the library's famous lions, Patience and Fortitude. I am happy to report they were a great hit and, fortunately, were left untouched during the week of the festivities. Each celebration was themed, and we hired a theatrical company that specialized in street performers to produce shows in the spirit of the theme. Particular favorites were fancifully dressed stiltwalkers and mimes who distributed perfume samples as they strolled through the crowds. Modern dance companies, accompanied by live music, charmed the enthusiastic audiences.

Mayor Koch's office lent its support thanks to one of the mayor's deputies, Herb Rickman, who at the time was charged with enlarging the importance of New York City as the fashion capital. He believed, as I did, that fragrance and fashion were symbiotic and deserved city hall's support not only because of the artistic nature of our industries but of their importance to the economy of the city. Herb arranged for the foundation to receive annual mayoral proclamations declaring the importance of Fragrance Week. He was usually on hand at the opening ceremonies each year to present the proclamation to the president of the foundation and members of the board. It certainly added authenticity to the event. In the mid-nineties, another member of the mayor's office of business development, Norman Silverberg, arranged for Fragrance Week to be featured on the Jumbotron in Times Square. It created quite a buzz. Department and specialty stores jumped on the bandwagon and became partners. Each interpreted the year's theme in-store for their shoppers. We worked closely with the display, promotion, and publicity staffs of the stores. Together, we created exclusive tie-ins with all our members (magazines, suppliers, and marketers). They provided experts to run the

Joining Lawrence Aiken, President, Sanofi and Eugene Grisanti, President, International Flavors & Fragrances.

specially conceived events for the week. Several of the stores placed charming flower carts, manned by models, in front of their entrances to herald the celebration. The models distributed gift cards, fragrance samples, and flowers.

To attract the uptown crowd, we moved the festivities to the much-admired plaza fountain and mini-park in front of the Plaza Hotel on Fifth Avenue and Fifty-Ninth Street. The perfumers of Givaudan-Roure, one of the industry's top fragrance creators, dreamed up a lovely spring bouquet to pour into the waters of the fountain and to distribute to the enthusiastic public. What really caused a sensation was a parade of flower-bedecked Central Park horse-drawn carriages carrying glamorous models down Fifth Avenue. They sprayed perfume in the air en route and distributed fragrance samples—serious traffic stoppers. Following performances and the presentations of the mayor's proclamation, Bud Lindsay hosted annual luncheon celebrations for members of the foundation in one of the elegant dining rooms at the Plaza.

The *New York Times* published a calendar of all the exciting happenings every year on the Monday of Fragrance Week to guide readers to the opening-day celebrations and tie-in activities in participating stores. Other member magazines participated, including *New York*, which hosted Fragrance Week breakfast kickoffs for participating retailers and marketers representing Fragrance Foundation member companies.

New Yorkers and tourists visited the stores in droves to receive fragrance gifts, have their fragrance personalities analyzed, and meet the magazines' beauty editors, who made personal appearances in the stores. People had their palms read to discover their fragrance types and received long-stemmed roses. Experts were always on hand to answer perfume questions. Colorful posters designed and produced by magazine-member art departments were also given to attendees during the opening-day festivities. They became collectors' items for many of the recipients.

By the time the nineties rolled around, ten years of successful Fragrance Weeks held in New York City morphed into annual national Fragrance Week festivities to be held in eleven cities across the United States every fall. Yearly themes were keyed to special events, demonstrations, and competitions. To assist us in coordinating activities with retailers, media, and city halls, we retained local PR firms.

One of the first National Fragrance Weeks saluted "American cities with the most beautiful and fragrant gardens." Leading retailers in each city participated, with festivities that benefitted local gardens, including sensory plantings for the blind. I was really up on the subject because of a request from the Brooklyn Botanic Garden in the early seventies to discuss its "fragrance garden for the blind." Established in 1955, the first ever to exist in the country, it was designed by renowned landscape architect Alice Recknagel. (The Fragrance Garden was named in her memory in 2001.) A representative of the Fragrance Garden reached out to me about the possibility of working with the foundation to explore the variety of flowers, plants, and herbs essential to the sensory pleasures of visitors. I was more than delighted to have our perfumers make suggestions. They quickly shared their choice of olfactory plantings which, not surprisingly, happen to also provide the essential ingredients perfumers depend upon. Candidates for having the most appealing sweet-smelling properties included verbena, heliotrope, ornamental flowering tobacco, and lavender. To appeal to the sense of touch, the perfumers proposed fragrant plants with scented leaves like rose geranium, sage, patchouli, and lemon verbena. Since culinary plants hold a special place in most perfumers' hearts and fragrance palettes, they were almost unanimous in their recommendations of clary sage, rosemary, basil, and spearmint.

I am happy to report that the broad variety of lovely flowery summer smell and touch experiences can still be found in the Brooklyn Botanic's Fragrance Garden. And they are wondrously planted with ever more intriguing sensory adventures.

News of our collaboration garnered great interest from other botanical gardens around the country, including the Staten Island Botanic Garden, which we also helped in developing their fragrance garden for the blind. All the garden representatives who contacted us were eager to have as much information as possible on designing the physical space and selecting plantings for their gardens. In response, we prepared a special leaflet detailing the techniques for developing a fragrance garden for the blind. It included suggested plantings, placement of Braille signage at a height that allowed easy access for visitors who might be in wheelchairs, operational details, and a rendering of the layout of the garden. It was an absolutely inspired and inspiring project.

During the foundation's Fragrance Week celebrations, many retailers invited customers to seminars focused on techniques of successful gardening, as well as lessons in the art of flower arranging. Individual garden installations were installed throughout many stores. Experts shared techniques of making potpourri and floral bouquets. Perfume-related book signings added to the fun. Personal appearances by famous perfumers lent credibility, as did contests to win botanical garden memberships and complimentary tours. Opening-day festivities included fragrance scavenger hunts, luncheons, and galas.

All participating stores distributed an informative, specially designed booklet we developed, tracing the times of each year when the most fragrant flowers were harvested around the world. I worked with Burpee Seed Company to donate "Tapestry of Fragrance Collection" kits to consumers, which contained seeds for planting flowers prized for their pungent aromas.

As interest in National Fragrance Week grew, opening day ceremonies continued to be organized for the public and were recognized by presentations of mayoral proclamations in participating cities. In New York, a legislative resolution was passed, designating "National Fragrance Week in New York State." It was adopted on May 18, 1993. This resolution called upon the legislative body and residents of the state to "acknowledge the enormous importance of the fragrance industry to our economy and overall quality of life."

It was lovely to join with author and raconteur Tom Wolfe.

Year after year, new concepts were developed to appeal to a nationwide audience. One of the most unique involved one of the fragrance industry's renowned perfume bottle and box designers, Georges Gotlib, president of his namesake firm. In cooperation with the foundation, he designed a shiny white lunch box–shaped cardboard container to hold perfume samples. He illustrated the box with an art deco-style perfume bottle. Inside the artwork of the domed stoppers, he cleverly interpreted the skyline of each participating city. All the bottles also featured a label design highlighting the specific "Scent-Sational City." The logo was incorporated in each city's National Fragrance Week materials too. The boxes were gifted to consumers throughout the week. News about the gifts and activities appeared in the press, and most cities ran ads in local newspapers. The public responded enthusiastically.

A funny thing happened at B. Altman's department store in New York City. There was such an overwhelming response by consumers, I received an emergency telephone call from the fragrance buyer who demanded the event be shut down before anyone was hurt. There were just too many people. What we finally did was put a time limit on the availability of the boxes. It helped, but the store was not interested in a repeat performance. How quaint that sounds in today's "catch-as-catch-can" retail world, where everything possible is done to encourage crowds, no matter how unruly, to storm the gates and grab all the sales merchandise they can. Black Friday injuries are legend.

At the twelfth annual Fragrance Week celebration in New York, our theme, "A New World Is in the Air," was the focus of attention at the United Nations. The foundation had been known to the UN since 1969, when I was invited to speak to delegates on the global contribution of fragrance ingredients to the perfume industry.

Fragrance Week at the UN opened with the international children's choral group of the International Studies Elementary School, PS 11, singing songs to the audience expressing a yearning for a new and better world. The children were all wearing costumes of their native lands. The fragrance supplier Roure hosted the week's opening luncheon at the United Nations, which honored the special activities taking place in the city during Fragrance Week. Fragrant international events and demonstrations were held in local department and specialty stores, tying in with our tribute to the United Nations. Marc Rosen designed a perfume bottle logo with an outline of the map of the world at the center that appeared on all materials developed for the week.

One of our great success stories was the creation of testing centers in department stores for the sense of smell during Fragrance Week in New York. The idea came to me one day while I was busing down Fifth Avenue. When we reached Fifty-Ninth Street and Fifth Avenue at the entrance to Central Park, I noticed a crowd had gathered next to a parked trailer. I decided to get off the bus and find out what was causing such a commotion. As it turned out, passersby were being offered the opportunity to have their hearing tested. The result was a New York–style bottleneck. Being smell-centric, I couldn't help but think that if people would stand in line to have their hearing tested, about which they certainly had a basic knowledge, imagine their reaction to a similar event that allowed them to test their sense of smell, about which they knew next to nothing, and cared even less.

To prepare for such an event, I contacted one of the doctors we funded, Dr. Anthony Synnott (see chapter XII), who agreed to survey 270 students and faculty at Concordia University in Montreal about which one of the five senses each felt was the most precious to them. Sight was overwhelmingly the most valued (80 percent), followed by touch (13 percent) and hearing (7 percent). Only 1 percent of the samples rated smell as the most precious sense. "The least valued sense—the one people felt they are most willing to lose if they have to lose one—was smell (55 percent), touch (5 percent), hearing (4 percent), and sight (2 percent)."

I met with several of the sensory psychologists we had also funded through the Sense of Smell Institute (see chapter XII), as well as perfumers whose companies were members of the foundation, to develop a test kit of fragrance ingredients and appropriate testing materials.

When we were ready, I approached Macy's in New York to ask if we could test the concept during an upcoming Fragrance Week celebration in the store. The store agreed, and we set up an area in the Fragrance Department, manned by a perfumer, a sensory psychologist, and someone (usually me) from the Fragrance Foundation. Crowds lined up immediately. Each person was given a questionnaire to answer about how well or poorly she or he was able to smell. I took a leaf out of Dr. Cain's experiments based on his research techniques at Yale (see chapter XII) and invited customers to sniff a variety of popular odors that had been sprayed on cotton balls placed inside paper cups.

After each analysis, shoppers received information about the sense of smell and exercises[1] to improve it. Macy's was delighted with the enthusiastic response, and as a result, we included the test in the Fragrance Week activities scheduled for the store and offered other stores across the country the opportunity to do the same in the upcoming Fragrance Weeks in their cities. I should mention that at the end of each of the tests, consumers were gifted with miniature perfume samples, which certainly added to the popularity of the event.

Nevermore!

National Fragrance Week continued to draw media attention, retail participation, and the public's embrace well into the nineties, but as we approached the new millennium, commitments from the stores, the magazines, and the fragrance marketers began to fade, and slowly but surely, the curtain came down. I am reminded of the famous observation by Lewis Carroll in his masterpiece, *Alice's Adventures in Wonderland*: " 'Begin at the beginning,' the king said gravely, 'and go till you come to the end; then stop.' "

---

1. Exercise Your Sense of Smell:

- Train your mind, not your nose.
- Most odors are perceived at an unconscious level. Thinking about the odors of familiar things brings about increased awareness.
- Smell often, but not a lot. Our noses fatigue easily. It is far better to smell in moderation, pause, then smell again.
- With different odors, you can smell alternately, and this will increase the perception of the differences between them.
- To refresh your nose, blow a small amount of air rapidly through your nose, back and forth for a few moments and then return to smelling.
- Create emotional associations with fragrance that make places and things more memorable.
- Vary fragrance types so that the sense of smell does not become bored.

- Do, but don't overdo. Create a perfect circle of fragrance approximately an arm's length from the body. Only those who step inside that circle should be aware of your fragrance.

Surprisingly, most of us possess a sense of smell that is equal in potential to that of many professionals. What a pity most people do so little to explore this potential.

XVI

Climbing Summit 2000

Favorite Co-conspirators

Howard Perlmutter, professor, Management and Social Architecture, Aresty Institute of Executive Education at Wharton

James Preston, CEO of Avon and former treasurer of the foundation

Daniel Stebbins, president of Dragoco and board member of the foundation

Jeanette S. Wagner, president of Estée Lauder International and former foundation chairman

Sally Yeh, executive vice president of Bijan Fragrances and foundation board member

Geoffrey Webster, president worldwide of Givaudan Roure Fragrances and foundation board member

Eugene Grisanti, chairman, CEO, and president of International Fragrances & Fragrances and foundation board member

Bobby Short, stage-and-cabaret star

Shirley Lord, beauty director of *Vogue* magazine

Geraldine O'Keefe, perfumer and copresident of the New School of Perfumery Arts

Robert Chavez, vice president, Cosmetics and Fragrances, Macy's Northeast

Ann Gottlieb, industry consultant

Joyce Roche, vice president, Product Marketing, Avon

All our knowledge begins with sense, proceeds then to understanding, and ends with reason, beyond which nothing higher can be discovered in the human mind.

—Immanuel Kant, The Critique of Pure Reason

s early as 1990, the coming of the third millennium was beginning to sow seeds of anxiety and nervous anticipation. Global soothsayers were moving front and center to mete out predictions of uncertainty and hi-tech upheavals, landing a mythical Y2K bug on our collective doorstep. I was in a crystal-ball mood myself, and began to wonder if and how an industry like mine should (or could) prepare for the changes that surely were inevitable. The Fragrance Foundation seemed the perfect vehicle to take the lead, and my team began to develop an outline for a possible conference to address the cross-cultural dilemmas awaiting us all. In discussions with the board, one of the members, Jeanette Wagner, president of Estée Lauder International Inc., proposed a possible alliance with the Lauder Fellowship in International Studies Program at the Wharton School at the University of Pennsylvania. She offered to find out who might be the appropriate person at Wharton to contact.

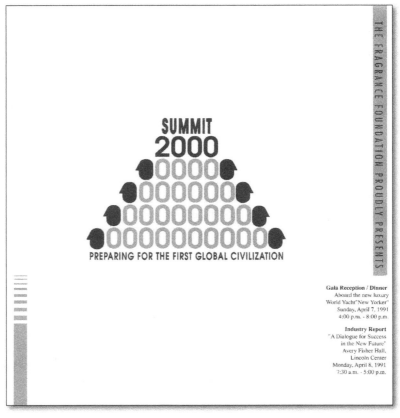

The Man of the Hour

In a matter of days, she identified Dr. Howard Perlmutter. I called him and set a meeting. I quickly realized we were kindred spirits. He was very enthusiastic about my proposed concept: "Summit 2000: Preparing for the First Global Civilization." He had, of course, been considering the coming challenges himself.

I explained we had visualized Summit 2000 as a two-phase conference. Phase I would take place at Wharton. It would not focus on the specific needs of the fragrance industry but rather on observations of a multidisciplinary, multicultural group of experts, including economists, environmentalists, and sociologists—as well as olfactory visionaries—who would help define new parameters for divining the future. Phase II would entail an in-depth repositioning of the information that was generated to reveal the major predictions that could affect the fragrance industry.

Dr. Perlmutter and I worked in tandem for over a year. When we were done, we had constructed a symposium that would be the first-ever funded by one US industry. It was carefully designed to prepare members to identify new global strategies for success in the fast-changing social, political, cultural, scientific, and technological climate in which they would have to survive—and hopefully prosper.

Celebrating with Dr. Howard Perlmutter and Folie Perlmutter with Dr. Fernando Aleu.

Phase I

A cross-section of the most advanced thinkers was invited by Dr. Perlmutter to join together at Wharton for a think tank. They generously shared their insights and projections for the future with a select audience, including several members of the Fragrance Foundation board: James Preston, Daniel Stebbins, Jeanette Wagner, Sally Yeh, Geoffrey Webster, and Eugene Grisanti, who also participated in one of the panel discussions. I have to admit I was disappointed that most of the members of the board did not attend.

Several days before leaving for Philadelphia to co-chair Summit 2000 with Dr. Perlmutter, my medical doctor revealed that a recent test I had taken revealed stage I breast cancer. It certainly was not welcome news. Nevertheless, I went to Philadelphia determined to carry on. The only person I talked to about it was Dr. Susan Schiffman, who assured me that a few weeks' delay in taking the next step was not critical.

When I returned from the conference, I went through a battery of tests, and the diagnosis was confirmed. It was time for a major decision: mastectomy or lumpectomy. Remember, this was 1991, and the benefits and challenges of each were still up for grabs. After sifting through all the alternatives and considerations regarding my ability to carry on with my work, I opted for the removal of the breast. Fortunately, the lymph nodes were not affected. The surgeon advised me I would be back on my feet in no time flat. Basically, I was, and I quickly moved forward with absolutely no side effects. Unfortunately, five years later, despite supposedly protective medication, I did have a recurrence and found myself following the same procedure that had allowed me to keep on keeping on in the first place. I never regretted the decisions. They allowed me to focus on what was important to me. I hardly missed a beat.

One of my first tasks on behalf of the summit was to coordinate the role of the brilliant futurist Edie Weiner, who had agreed to participated in Phase I with her equally talented colleague, Arnold Brown. It was their chore to interpret the information generated at the summit in conjunction with my staff and fourteen members of a fragrance industry summit advisory committee. Conclusions were to be presented at a full-day conference in New York at Lincoln Center. The goal was to encourage the industry to take the long view and begin the process that would result in moving from the here and now to a new and increasingly complex sensory world.

Phase II

The program presented at Lincoln Center was an historic exchange of information by twenty-seven visionaries from a broad spectrum of disciplines, including members of the Fragrance Foundation. The speakers were committed to examining the shape of the future, focusing on five crucial areas of change: global marketing, the uncertain consumer, social disruptions and technological reverberations, the changing corporate environment, and the worldwide sensory revolution.

A preconference celebration for attendees and speakers was launched aboard the world yacht *New Yorker*. A balloon-festooned gangplank welcomed the guests. Inside the main deck, the spirit of the occasion was captured by an abstract sculpture titled *Reflections of the Future*. It was designed by artist Eileen Ibrany in Lucite, glass, and mirrors, featuring futuristic mobiles holding perfume miniatures of member companies of the Fragrance Foundation. An array of small international flags were also placed strategically throughout the sculpture.

While the guests dined, danced, and enjoyed the breathtaking sunset views of the New York skyline and the Statue of Liberty, the 308-foot, four-deck cruiser made its way around Manhattan. When everyone disembarked, they received the official Summit 2000 T-shirt, sponsored by *GQ* and *Self* magazines.

Philippine-born Hector Cruz, a seventh-semester graphic design student at the Fashion Institute of Technology, was chosen to design the Summit 2000 logo for the Fragrance Foundation. A dramatic, futuristic, computer-graphic pyramid, it used "2000" as a decorative element, bookended by android symbols encircled by a bull's-eye graphic of fourteen challenging areas of change and concern:

Globalization	Stewardship
Multinational	Aroma-chology
Ecology	Interdependence
Insularity	Artificial Reality

Diversity	Soft Power
Quality	Safety
Empowerment	Customization

The logo appeared on all materials for the landmark event.

Indoctrinating the Industry

When media and members of the foundation gathered at Avery Fisher Hall at Lincoln Center the next day, Dr. Fernando Aleu accepted a mayoral proclamation from Susan Glickman, the assistant commissioner, from the Office of Business Development of the City of New York. The proclamation declared the week of April 8 Summit 2000 Week in New York City.

Key board members attended and participated, including Dr. Aleu, Eugene Grisanti, James Preston, Jeanette Wagner, and Sally Yeh.

Among the olfactory scientists who made presentations were Dr. Gary Beauchamp, director of the Monell Chemical Senses Center; Dr. Dunio Yamazaki, associate member of Monell; Dr. William H. Redd, attending psychologist, Memorial Sloan Kettering Cancer Center; and Dr. Susan Schiffman, professor of medical psychology at Duke University Hospital and chairperson of the Scientific Advisory Committee of the Fragrance Research Fund.

Speaking Out

In opening the conference in New York, Dr. Perlmutter announced, "This first symposium, focusing on a global civilization, is being produced because of increasing global interdependencies in the political, economic, social cultural, scientific, technological, medical, and ecological arenas of society. We also see in the emergence of this new type of civilization enormous positive implications for improving the quality of human life through these syncretisms with special potential for the human senses of smell, touch, sound, sight, and taste."

Jeanette Wagner reminded the audience that "by applying one new—even revolutionary—idea for change in your own organization, by becoming obsessed with the need for change in meeting the challenges of the decade, you will not wait for the future to overtake you—you will invent the future yourself."

Following her remarks, authorities from within and outside the industry joined four-member panel discussions. Each panel was led by a moderator. The first focused on "Markets Without Walls":

Beware of anything that was written or said a few years ago— markets have a habit of surprising with swift changes.
—George Fields, chairman and CEO,
ASI Marketing Research (Japan)

The twenty-first century will see a development of buying groups, cooperatives, and wholesaler-supported chains to allow independent retailers to remain competitive.
—Thomas Rauh, director of retail consulting, Ernst &
Young

Yes, in the year 2000, real history and deep culture will be the roots of all success, and any perfume will be in itself a story, a history, a novel, a written novel. Legitimacy will be deep, philosophical. Managers of the year 2000 will essentially be men and women of culture.
—Christian Blanckaert, president, Comité Colbert

"Selling the New Who" was the point of discussion of the second panel:

We live in an opaque world where marketers increasingly have to struggle to discover the true nature of the consumer in order not to get lost. Tracking the new consumer now requires moving pictures, not snapshots.
—Arnold Brown, chairman, Weiner Edrich Brown

Lifestyles and life stages have become less predictable. You can't tell as much about people as you used to simply by knowing their age, gender, how much they make, or where they live. You have to understand how all of these "particle markets" fit together to form the individual consumer.
—Diane Crispell, contributing editor, *American Demographics*

The spread of Western culture, or coming to be of the global civilization, would appear to be resulting in the universalization of a regime of olfactive silence or neutrality and the standardization of a growing number of associations between certain scents and concepts. But this development is provoking counter-reactions as well.
—David Howes, professor, Dept. of Sociology and Anthropology, Concordia University

The global media is now, for better or for worse, a genie that would never—and could never—be stuffed back into the bottle from which it came.
—Bernard Leser, president, Condé Nast Publications

The challenges of "Living on the Edge" took center stage next:

Given the impressiveness of our knowledge and power, can we maintain respect for the natural and social world?
—Ilene Leff, president, International Management Consultants

As society evolves and new stresses and pressures are added to its fabric, technology and science will be called upon to play increasingly greater roles in defining our human environment and in enhancing our appreciation of life and our potential of overcoming natural or manmade adversity.
—Dr. Anthony Tomazinis, professor of city and regional planning, director of Translab, University of Pennsylvania

The black-and-white, sensory-deprived world of the intellect created by the printing press will give way to multisensory, animated, physically interactive forms of knowledge in the future. Information will be less conceptual and more perceptual.
—Dr. Myron Krueger, president, Artificial Reality

The very growth of high-tech computerization is a major factor in our society's dehumanization. Everyone seems delighted by our technological strides, but its side effect may well be the destruction of human communication!
    —Letitia Baldrige, president, Letitia Baldrige Enterprises

The use of scent within the context of magic has an ancient history which will gradually become more mainstream as the fragrance archetypes for image, sophistication, power and sexual attraction are complimented by the use of fragrance to assist in deep personal transformation. A specific scent can become an aromatic beacon for a desired process of change when coupled with magical intention and imagination.
    —John Steele, aromatic consultant, Lifetree Aromatix

A revealing discussion revolved around "Redefining Corporate Culture":

The overriding value will be integrity, not just quality. Quality is an economic concept that measures and strives for a flawless product. Integrity is an ethical and moral approach to everything done from beginning to end to satisfy many stakeholder groups in the face of stiffened and smartened competition.
    —Edith Weiner, president, Weiner Edrich Brown

The corporation of the future has the mission of addressing specific community needs to design and implement programs which offer opportunities for enriched life, and which provide members of a community with skills, knowledge, and assistance to accomplish positive social goals.
    —Lee Kennedy, director of 3M's corporate marketing service

The twenty-first-century enterprise is expected to be global in perspective and in the scope of operations. It will be innovative and

entrepreneurial focused on value-added quality and time-based competition.
—Dr. Jerry Wind, Lauder professor and professor of marketing, director of SEI Center for Advanced Studies in Management, the Wharton School, University of Pennsylvania

The old models of leadership won't fit the bill. There will be a need for leaders not managers, command and control vs. participative expatriates vs. nationals and vertical integration vs. partnerships with suppliers and customers.
—Robert Roseillo, principal, McKinsey & Co.

There will be a need for greater flexibility in job design in the corporation of the future. The individual employee will need to understand how he/she fits into the composite picture and how his/her function contributes to the whole. ... Corporations will have to nurture loyalty and create the perception from the employee's perspective that he/she is a long-term investment. One way this can be accomplished is with a mentor program that will personalize the junior executive's experience and give the senior manager exposure to the front line.
—Mary Minowalda and Jane Page, graduate students at the Wharton School, University of Pennsylvania

And finally, it was time to examine "Sensory Experiences in the Twenty-First Century":

This century will be marked by coordination and fusion of all the senses—sight, sound, touch, taste and smell, into entire integrated functional experiences. This will affect our lifestyles, our work and our play.
—Eugene P. Grisanti, chairman, CEO, and president of International Flavors & Fragrances and member of the board of the Fragrance Foundation and Fragrance Research Fund

We must plan now for the large future population of independent affluent older consumers who will want to feel good about themselves and with others.
—Dr. Barbara Silverstone, executive director, the Lighthouse

Odors play a major role in mood. They can reduce feelings of depression and promote relaxation. Psychotherapeutic methods incorporating the use of fragrance will become more important in the twenty-first century.
—Dr. Susan Schiffman, professor of medical psychology, Duke Medical Center, Duke University Hospital, and chairperson of the Fragrance Research Fund Scientific Committee

The role of odor is a key element in the presentation of the self and in inter-personal communication. The corollary of this role is the importance of odor in the moral construction of the other and the definitional process itself.
—Dr. Anthony Synnott, professor, Department of Sociology and Anthropology, Concordia University, Canada

A pleasing scent will certainly help set a pleasurable mood. ... It can and will direct the mind into positive thought and behavior. ... It can reduce stress and anxiety.
—Dr. Jack Mausner, senior vice president of research and development, Chanel Inc., and president of the Fragrance Research Fund

A vigorous and insightful Q&A session, followed by a luncheon, completed the morning portion of the program. The second half of the conference opened with presentations of scrolls of recognition for the two winning Fragrances of the Future. Fifteen suppliers of the Fragrance Foundation each submitted two avant-garde fragrances—one for women and one for men. There was a prestigious panel of six judges: Bobby Short, Shirley Lord, Geraldine O'Keefe, Robert Chavez, Ann Gottlieb, and Joyce Roche.

At the conclusion of the summit, all the attendees received a twelve-year miniature pocket calendar, "Creating Memories for the 21st Century." It fanned out to reveal each year, including national holidays and important dates.

In a charming "bread and butter" letter from Letitia Baldrige, written to me a couple of days after the conference, she opined:

> As an all-time pro in the business, I marveled at the way you handled all of us for twenty-four hours! The movement of people, the boat trip (on a perfect day), and the symposium itself were handled with utmost efficiency and grace, kindness, and style.
>
> Dr. Aleu was perfect—amiable, brilliant, and witty. You, however, were the Queen of the Day and Night. I laud you, congratulate you, and hope you are on vacation right at this minute. Thanks for having me!

Revisiting Summit 2000

For those members of the industry who, for one reason or another, did not attend the summit and expressed concern at having missed this information-packed milestone, we periodically strove to revisit the treasure trove of revelations presented at Wharton and Lincoln Center. A perfect example was the conference the Globalization of the Senses, which we held six years later at the Plaza Hotel in New York. Several of the summit participants joined the conference, including Dr. Howard V. Perlmutter, who again was our keynote speaker, in his new capacity as emeritus professor of social architecture and management at the Wharton School, University of Pennsylvania:

> The globalization of the senses help us to build, bridge, and bond between areas of the world and the subcultures that are involved. A global civilization is emerging slowly and executives need to learn three main things in order to succeed in this new civilization:
>
> • Develop a mind-set so you can make sense of 95 percent of what you read about events happening around the world and on the planet.

- Develop global business literacy. Understand how business is evolving globally and how people compete and cooperate; find their niches; or lose their companies worldwide.
- Develop cross-cultural competencies; the capacity to move anywhere in the world and to cross cultural divides and build relationships which involve minimally, trust and respect.

A series of panel discussions followed. Among the highlights were observations by Cathy Yohalem, CEO of C-Source Communications LLC, a Coopers and Lybrand Company: "Technology is the powerful enabler that is allowing us to respond to information faster than ever before, in 'real time.' "

She urged executives to think "in a nonlinear, out-of-the-box fashion. Today, in order to compete, businesses need to know the various markets being influenced by the internet." She pinpointed one-to-one marketing to access the consumer; business-to-business connections to interact with their partners, suppliers, or vendors; and strategic technology options to create new visions for the future.

Yves de Chiris, vice president of Fine Fragrance Worldwide, Quest International Inc., encouraged the audience to take a world view and asked, "What makes a global fragrance?" His answer: "By using information technology to structure and analyze consumer research."

Five years ago Quest International initiated the MIRIAD system featuring the art of understanding the consumer. MIRIAD stands for "Multimedia Initiative Redefining Intelligent Aromatic Design." This system incorporates six perfumery and marketing tools: perfume planets, or fragrance genealogy; perfume pulse, a qualitative consumer research program; association testing, a qualitative market research program with a broad global reach that can determine fragrance preferences worldwide; product tracking, an international retrieval system for both geographic markets and fragrance brands; a fragrance futurology program to determine future consumer attitudes and values and how these relate to fragrance; and Lignes de Force, a method by which one can visualize how a fragrance smells. The MIRIAD system can also be adjusted to take on new tools.

A special video was shown that previewed Quest's remarkable Fragrance Exploratorium, an interactive display designed to simulate all the senses.

A provocative presentation, "Kansai: The Harmonic Balances of All the Senses," was the centerpiece of remarks by Dr. Clifford R. Bragdon, vice president of the National Aviation and Transportation Center and dean of the School of Aviation Transportation, Dowling College:

> The concept of sensory wholeness, or Kansai, represents a harmony among the five senses, rather than dominance of any individual sense. This sensory-balanced approach has traditionally evaded those professions responsible for planning and designing our cities. The success of the future requires unlocking all five senses in understanding the functionality of the city, thereby creating a sensory master plan.
>
> Aroma is now gaining recognition as an environmental attribute capable of enhancing efficiency, safety, and enjoyment. Aroma-based aspects of environmental transportation research have already been initiated at the NAT Center in terms of human factors. Various types of diffuser systems will be investigated in terms of specific tasks to determine the influence of aroma as a means to enhance safety, vigilance, and human performance.
>
> Aroma-chology is an essential sensory ingredient that will grow in importance to help us find solutions for today's problems to make our tomorrows better.

The olfactory dimension in modern and contemporary art was the imaginative subject of James Drobnick, assistant editor of *Parachute Art* magazine and member of the faculty of Concordia University:

> Contemporary artists are incorporating scents into their work in a manner unprecedented in the history of art. Here are a few qualities of scent that have compelled artists to create fragrant works of art:

- Intimacy: Artworks that immerse the viewer in fragrance to foster an engagement that is physical, intimate, yet subliminal. An example of an artist who incorporates fragrances and intimacy is Wolfgang Laib.

- Intensity: Artists seek out odors because they are highly charged with personal associations, many of which may be unconscious to gallery-goers until isolated and presented. Dennis Oppenheimer, for example, unites fragrance and intensity in his artwork.
- Interactivity: when inhaling aromas, audiences become aware of their own bodies and relation in space. Art becomes social and highlights notions of community and cultural differences. The works of Rirkrit Tiravanija often combine interactivity and fragrance. Artists can enhance awareness about the multiple roles that scent can play in other lives.

Dr. Rachel Herz, assistant member of Monell, Chemical Senses Center, directed her remarks to the interrelationship of olfaction and music: "Music and odors are both rich in evocative and emotional properties and have perceptual and experiential qualities that make them highly compatible." In order to describe the perceptual and cognitive synergism that occurs when odor and music are combined, Dr. Herz coined the term "smellody." She went on to say:

The two most important variables that mediate the smellody, or odor and music interaction, are the familiarity and pleasantness of the music and odor. If the odor is pleasant, the music will be perceived as more pleasant than it would alone. If the odor is unpleasant, the music will be perceived as less pleasant than it would alone.

There are many ways that music and odor influence each other and enhance the quality of both moment to moment experiences and long term remembrances. … It only takes a little creativity and some basic knowledge to take advantage of these sensory effects and produce a powerful and memorable experience.

Karyn Khoury, vice president, Corporate Fragrance Development Worldwide, Estée Lauder Companies Inc., shared her vision of the importance of multisensory fragrance creation:

Today's creative challenge, and the key to global success, is to preserve the perfumery artistry and creativity while serving the business need.

The industry needs to reexamine its long-standing beliefs about which types of fragrance and which of its attributes are appropriate for which markets.

The industry also needs to find more effective ways of reaching the consumer. This can be done by activating multiple senses through fragrance. It is important to provide multiple, universally understood appeals which remain consistent throughout the world, while allowing individual interpretation based on personal and cultural preferences.

A deliberately multisensory approach to fragrance creation can help us to develop distinctive yet universal fragrances which reach the global consumer in new, more direct and more powerful ways. And the results can give the consumers a richer deeper, more multidimensional fragrance experience.

Dr. Myron W. Krueger, president of Artificial Reality Corp., Sensory Software: Sight, Touch, Hearing and Smell, explained that adding olfactory stimuli to virtual reality came to him as a result of his participation at Summit 2000. It started him thinking about the possibilities of the body itself as a sense:

In order to properly combine all the senses in the simulated or virtual world, it's necessary to perfect the olfactory component. To do this, I suggest the creation of an olfactory superscent, or an artificial instrument for detecting odor. This instrument would bring to the study of olfaction what the microscope, telescope, sonar and seismograph have brought to their respective fields.

The goal is making a virtual odor that stands for a real odor. In the near future many of the improvements to the simulation in the "virtual world" will assist us with daily activities in the real world.

Looking back at the amazing insights shared by the experts at Wharton and Lincoln Center, it is remarkable to realize that much of what they predicted has come to pass. The summit was a once-in-a-lifetime experience. Whether it (and follow-up presentations) inspired the industry to change its trajectory is still an open question.

XVII

Shadows in the City of Light

Favorite Co-conspirators

Susan Schiffman, professor, Department of Psychiatry, Duke University School of Medicine

David Howes, associate professor, Department of Sociology and Anthropology, Concordia University in Canada

Nicky Kinnard, managing director, Space NK Apothecary[1]

Odile Lobadowsky, director general, Kenzo Parfums

Marie Dumont, general manager, L'Artisan Parfumeur

Dr. Luca Turin, chief scientist, Flexitral Inc.

Patrick Bousquet-Chavanne, president of Estée Lauder USA and chairman of Fragrance Foundation board

Alain Grange Cabanne, president, French Federation of Perfumery and Cosmetics

Memories, imagination, old sentiments, and associations are more readily reached through the sense of smell than through any other channel.

—Oliver Wendell Holmes

There was good news and bad news waiting for me and my staff (Mary Ellen Lapsansky, Terry Molnar, and Lilia Nicoletti) when we flew to Paris in October 2002.

We had two objectives. The first was to prepare for an international symposium, Well-Being, Aroma-Chology, and the Future of Fragrance, which the Fragrance Foundation was producing with financial support of several supplier members, including Givaudan; International Flavors & Fragrances; Firmenich; Dragoco; Quest; the Cosmetic, Toiletry, and Fragrance Association; Sense of Smell Institute; and *Beauty Fashion* magazine. The second was to attend ceremonies at the Paris city hall, Ville de Paris, where I was to have the great honor of receiving the silver Medal of the City of Paris.

Mary Ellen and I had held meetings in Paris during the year before the symposium was scheduled to take place with industry associations, including the French Federation of Perfumery and Cosmetics, as well as the International Duty Free Travel Retailer. We received commitments from each to support the symposium with attendance by their members. This was critical because we were not confident of how many US companies would attend, and we were depending on the European industry to make up the difference. Wrong! Despite verbal commitments, the attendance was below our expectations. We anticipated five hundred, but when the dust settled, we welcomed three hundred delegates representing thirteen countries around the globe. Extraordinary speakers, recognized for their futuristic thinking, arrived from Europe and the United States, and the stage was set for a high-powered, hi-tech audiovisual presentation. In-depth materials were distributed to everyone attending. I was the interlocutor, and as the program rolled out, I realized our creation, despite the smaller attendance, had the earmarks of a once-in-a-lifetime undertaking.

The symposium was keyed to the future of fragrance, the new science of Aroma-chology (see chapter XII), which was based on studies supported by the Sense of Smell Institute of the mind-body connection. It was conceived to help the fragrance industry gain a strong foothold in the emerging global concern for well-being. Our UK trade media partner was *Esprit* magazine, and the following observations include excerpts of coverage by its editor, Jonathan Charles:

> In speeches on the mind-body-fragrance connection, delegates heard that smell is used democratically by the brain in its multisensory approach to analyzing messages, recalling experiences and prioritizing action. By focusing its communications to consumers on one principal message—that fragrance is sexy—the industry, it was argued, is limiting the range of possibilities open to it and severely restricting the potential size of its commercial market.

One of the highlights of the symposium was the presentation by Olwen Wolfe, president of Worlding, a Paris-based intercultural strategic consultancy, who revealed the results of her landmark qualitative research study, commissioned by the Fragrance Foundation, to examine "Consumer Perceptions and Expectations of Fragrance and Well-Being." Seven countries were included in the survey: USA, France, Italy, Spain, Germany, the United Kingdom, and Japan. The study analyzed the differences and similarities between seven cultures and took eighteen months to complete. The findings were based on detailed in-the-home interviews with one hundred women aged between fifteen and fifty-five from a wide range of social and demographic categories.

Comparisons of what the interviewees said and what they actually did were carefully monitored. The study found that fragrance and a sense of well-being were intrinsically linked to the global consumer's quest for individualism and the search for social appropriateness, self-confidence, and personal identity against a background of increasing stress, anxiety, depression, information overload, and excess of choice. It demonstrated people's personal need for fragrances that they found sexy but also comforting—a survival tool against the pressures of urban life. Women's reaction to fragrances was shown to differ depending on age and stage of life, whether they were about to leave home for the first time, were newly pregnant, or undergoing menopause. This, Owen Wolfe suggested, presented fragrance companies with the opportunity to communicate aspects of their brands that would most appeal to a particular life stage. For example, she proposed, marketers might promote the essential oil elements of fine fragrances to pregnant women who have a heightened awareness of the importance of well-being.

Dr. Susan Schiffman explored the frontiers of the mind-body-fragrance connection, and Dr. David Howes, coauthor of *A Cultural History of Smell*, both supported Olwen's findings with further evidence of how certain odors promote relaxation, reduce stress, and treat pain both psychologically and physically.

In a speech devoted to marketing societal trends, Barbara Busch, president of Analysis, the Scent Company International, urged the delegates to dare to be different. "We must search for deeper values," she said. "Newness is no longer the reason to purchase." This philosophy was expanded upon during the presentations on strategies for success in

"Marketing the Sense of Smell at Retail," presented by the highly successful threesome Nicky Kinnard, Odile Lobadowsky, and Marie Dumont.

Dr. Luca Turin, chief scientist at Flexitral Inc., said that new theories on how the brain detects smell, focusing on molecular vibration rather than molecular shape, was providing the impetus behind the development of new aroma chemicals that should lead to exciting new products in the future. Helen Fisher, a research professor in the Department of Anthropology at Rutgers University and author of *The First Sex: The Natural Talents of Women and How They Are Changing the World*, stressed that we are now moving toward a more collaborative world in which women share economic power, and as pregnancy rates fall in the Western world below population replacement, women have become far more sexual creatures, enjoying more love, romance, lust, and attachments. This was a theme echoed both by Sebastian De Diesbach, president of Promostyle, a fashion and design forecasting company, and Nelly Rodi, president of Nelly Rodi, Agence de Style, a fashion design agency, who agreed "people are living for the moment. They see life as a feast to enjoy now." Both stressed that "time is precious and energy is the keyword for the future." How prescient they all were.

The keynote speaker at the luncheon was the charismatic Peter Goldmark, who at the time was chairman and CEO of the *International Herald Tribune*. He spoke brilliantly of "changes and challenges in the global community within the context of our increasingly uncertain world."

This extraordinary gathering of experts set the stage for greater understanding of the market potential of fragrances that would provide emotional comfort, help reduce stress, energize, and improve interpersonal relationships. I must confess the industry never really did embrace the difference between the folklore of aromatherapy and the solid science of Aroma-chology in marketing fragrance. What they did do, in the main, was increasingly adopt the research, which resulted in a wide variety of more scientifically based products and practices which, of course, is a good thing.

The event received audience raves and excellent news coverage. When all was said and done, despite the limited audience and reduced revenue, the consensus was that we had fulfilled our goal to present inspiring new tools for future global success.

Vive la France

The trip took a very glamorous turn thanks to a grand decision by the French to present the Medal of the City of Paris to me at ceremonies to be held in the magnificent city hall, Hotel de Ville. Woody Allen couldn't have written a more dreamlike scenario. From start to finish, it was pure fantasy. A bright sunny morning set the mood, as did the arrival of a sleek black limo to pick me up at the Intercontinental Hotel. I was joined by my Fragrance Foundation colleagues, as well as Michele Meyer (a member of the board of the French Fragrance Foundation), who I suspected was the person who had proposed the idea of honoring me to the powers in charge.

Arriving at city hall, we were stopped by the elegantly uniformed guards on duty at the VIP driveway. Once we were identified, the guards ceremoniously waved us into the inner sanctum of the building. It was an awesome moment. Once inside, we were surrounded by the majesty of France. A soaring space, defined by majestic columns, provided the backdrop for a dramatic staircase covered in plush royal red carpeting. At the top of the stairs, we were received in a grand reception hall where the medal would be formally presented. Many of the members of the French fragrance industry, as well as colleagues from the United States, were in attendance, including Patrick Bousquet-Chavanne, president of Estée

Michele Meyer, a special French friend.

Lauder USA and chairman of the Fragrance Foundation board, and Alain Grange Cabanne.

Lyne Cohen-Solal, deputy mayor of the city of Paris, in charge of the arts and crafts industry, welcomed me and offered a handsome gold-and-brown chair for me to sit on until the ceremonies began. She noted in true Parisian style that the gold-trimmed brown two-piece knit I was wearing not only matched my chair but the room. We both laughed at the coincidence. A few moments later, the deputy mayor opened the ceremonies. In her remarks, she saluted my "commitment over the past twelve years to the fragrance world's formidable Franco/American relationship."

The medal, featuring a sailing ship on one side, "symbolized Paris as unsinkable," explained Mme Cohen-Solal. "Seas may get rough, and the boat may rock from side to side, but it will never sink." My kind of boat!

I was deeply touched and said so: "I will always treasure this moment and the medal, which exemplifies for me a lifetime love affair with the French people and perfume."

A lavish cocktail reception followed the ceremonies. The icing on the cake, as the unforgettable affair ended, was an extravagant bouquet of flowers. Ah! The French!

---

1. Space NK was established in 1993 with the opening of its first store in Covent Garden, London. It would owe its success to positioning the company as the launch pad for young British and European designers. Today, it retails leading niche designer brands from all over the world.

XVIII

Future Tense

The whole secret of life is to be interested in one thing profoundly and in a thousand things well.
—**Horace Walpole**

As I put the finishing touches on my reminiscences, how exhilarating it is to know that I will always have the memory of my forty years in the wonderland of the senses: No matter where I go, what I do, and how things change, my memory bank is overflowing with emotional capital. I decided to spend it in praise of creativity, passion with a purpose, and the joys and rewards of being interested in "one thing profoundly."

Total recall is a tricky business, but I have the advantage of being a lifelong hoarder, accumulating voluminous files filled to overflowing with letters, articles, and speeches (written by me and others), and a treasure trove of photographs, all of which have helped me keep most of my memories from slipping and sliding away.

Curiosity, flexibility, and passion were constant companions on my journey from scents to the senses. I thrived in a privileged, sensory-charged world peopled by the most provocative, supportive talents. Their emotional largesse taught me how to fly, live under water when necessary, and encouraged me to be the heroine of my own story. It proved to be an unbeatable combination.

Metamorphosis Unbound

During my forty years with the Fragrance Foundation, the small half-million-dollar fragrance industry of the sixties blasted through the billion-dollar mark; a vast array of talented women filled leadership positions at every level of management; the scientific community doubled down on the importance of the sense of smell to well-being; media coverage expanded in every conceivable medium from tech to type (the Perfumed Plume Award honoring editorial diversity was launched in 2016 by my former associate, Mary Ellen Lapsansky); a stunning array of scent-related environmental developments challenged the status quo; an ever-increasing number of bachelor's and master's degree graduates from the Fashion Institute of Technology majored in beauty and fragrance marketing and product development; a dazzling variety of new scent sensations from designers, celebrities, and fine fragrance houses made headlines around the world; and the appearance of perfume bottles—historical and contemporary—continue to receive star billing in major museum exhibitions, including the 2015 blockbuster exhibition, *China Through the Looking Glass*, at the Metropolitan Museum of Art in New York. The pull and power of the FiFi (the famous nickname was inexplicably dropped several years ago) still has no expiration date. Will it continue to fulfill its destiny as the crème de la crème of fragrance excellence? That is a question still to be answered.

No matter how perfectly the stars may be aligned, back here on terra firma, it is crystal clear there is no straight line to Nirvana. Even when it is in sight, endless ups, downs, and roundabouts challenge and define us. Did I keep my balance against even the gustiest of headwinds? Almost always. Was I ever disappointed or frustrated? Absolutely. Did I get what it takes to meet the insistence of constant change by changing? Usually. Do I have regrets? A few. Were my dreams fulfilled? Definitely! I can honestly say dedicating myself to the understanding and appreciation of the pleasures of the senses, with emphasis on the wonders of scent, led me to my own version of Nirvana.

Ticking Time Clock

As the new century picked up steam, thoughts of retirement began to settle into my consciousness. I was inspired by the wisdom of the sixties communication guru, Marshall McLuhan: "Control over change would seem to consist in moving not with it but ahead of it" (*Understanding Media*, 1964). That is certainly what I had in mind when I wrote to the board of my desire to step down in 2003. Even though I had just celebrated my seventy-eighth birthday, I still felt capable of carrying on physically, emotionally, and intellectually. Nevertheless, I believed it was time. In fact, I remember when the fashion designer Bill Blass described retirement (which he did in 1999) as "knowing when to leave the party." I made a mental note to do the same. The decisive factor for me, however, was the make-or-break social dynamics I felt were about to impact the industry. I considered it a matter of grace to pass the torch to successors who I hoped could and would jump into the fray with avant-garde know-how, eager and ready to address come what may.

I thought the jury was out, but there was good news at the dawn of 2018. The Board of Directors of the Fragrance Foundation appointed a remarkably dedicated and insightful new president, Linda Levy. The prognosis: full-speed ahead. Feels like a miracle in the making.

Poetic Justice

All changes, even the most longed for, have their melancholy. What we leave behind is a part of ourselves; we must die to one life before we can enter another.
—Anatole France

I could certainly relate to these words of wisdom. Though I was prepared for my new future, the transition turned out to be difficult for reasons I hadn't anticipated. During a two-year consultancy, the well-honed operations of the foundation were methodically disassembled. Nothing was sacrosanct. I found myself sleeping less and worrying more. I discussed my concern with one of the members of the board who advised me in no uncertain terms, "Stop worrying about the Fragrance Foundation. It is not your responsibility anymore. Just take care of yourself." I was startled. There was no way I could close the foundation out of my heart. Yet, after a few months, I recognized the reality of what he had said and refocused on my planned transition to a new center of gravity.[1] Once and for all, I cleared my head of years of achievements, honors, and fulfillments. They are just sweet memories now.

Past Tense

Not that I haven't occasionally enjoyed a backward glance. I still savor the memories of lessons learned. It was in those halcyon days my assorted talents and skills found their voice. Once I fell in love with the world of scents, I drew on what I knew. Even the most difficult questions seemed to be transparent. Most answers had become hardwired. My successes were built on what I had already achieved. What made the difference was my determination to meet changing demands dictated by an endless variety of circumstances, storylines, and a cast of thousands. The more I think about it, I can't help but wonder: Of all that was accomplished, what is even remotely replicable, rethinkable, or simply toss-outable.[2] Not that it really matters. It's yesterday's news.

Perhaps the takeaway, after all is said and done, is having the ability to maintain a mind-set that is always open to change, no matter how disruptive. The Buddhists call it "being awake." A good idea, too, for those of us living in the hi-tech twenty-first century. This old world is nothing like what it was when I retired just twelve short years ago. Computers and their offspring—the internet, smartphones, iPads, apps, and emojis—rule our lives. A whole new silent language has had a rather robotic effect on our ability to communicate with one another face-to-face. The almost total absorption in our iPhones defies reason. Walking down the street, in restaurants, trains, buses, automobiles, and even at concerts, sports events, and the theater, we are shackled, willingly, to a new and totally demanding lover. Too many of us reach out to the world through symbols (shades of hieroglyphics), sending emails and text messages that mangle the English language. There is a universe of perfectly reasonable people who now turn to blogs, Facebook, LinkedIn, Twitter, Pinterest, and Instagram for instant gratification, information, guidance, approval, and friends they may or may not ever see.

And then there is the workplace. Article after article has appeared in the most prestigious media blasting the corporate world for making their offices, factories, showrooms, and factories so inhospitable that an overwhelming number of workers hate their jobs (if they can find them!)

213

and feel undervalued and definitely expendable. All this to say nothing of the burnout caused by round-the-clock expectations engendered by technology that never rests and keeps the workers of the world on call wherever they may be at any hour of the day or night. As far as the retail community is concerned, millennials are "in" and the rest of us are apparently "out" as business struggles with changes so dynamic that even the fate of brick-and-mortar stores lies in the balance. It all takes your breath away.

True or False?

Of course, there have always been those who believe true change is a figment of the imagination. The most famous doubter was the nineteenth-century Frenchman Jean-Baptiste Alphonse Karr,[3] whose lament on the subject is still quoted today: "The more things change, the more they stay the same." What I wouldn't give to hear this cynic's take on our topsy-turvy digital age.

Shakespeare Was Right!

Yes, we are still the players in life's stories, but globalization has thrust us onto a very crowded, far-flung hi-tech stage. How we each interpret our parts is a very fascinating bit of theater. For those of us on a career path, reaching stardom is the goal. But for a lifetime of fulfillment beyond the applause, one has to start with a full heart capable of bringing the highest degree of excellence to the endless changes required. I have always found inspiration embedded in the magical panorama of the arts. There, in plain sight, are the artists, musicians, and performers who never lose touch with the power of their senses. They spend 24/7 defining and redefining their talents to the nth degree. Money is rarely the question. Time is irrelevant. Their goal is to help the rest of us find our way through a sensory-deprived inner landscape that may sometimes be puzzling but can be transformative if we allow it. That is surely the goal of all creative spirits, whether they are in starring roles or members of the supporting cast.

In my case, the drama of it all demanded a high-wire performance each and every day. I never saw my role as confrontational. Neither protagonist nor antagonist, I preferred to be firmly set in the exact middle, not tilting to the left or right, without prejudice or favoritism. It didn't always satisfy the interests of some. What I believe worked for me was being blessed with extraordinary energy and a singular determination to inspire and energize the fragrance industry and the public—day in, day out.

Trade Secrets

It absolutely takes courage, stamina, ingenuity, intuition, and a sense of humor to be ready at any moment to get ahead of the changes bearing down on all of us. From my point of view, it helps, too, to develop the intuitive sixth sense. Imagine being able to hear the grass growing. I was alerted to the unlikely possibility by a child psychologist I interviewed in the fifties.[4] My involvement with fragrance and the sense of smell heightened my sensitivity to the power of all the senses. I taught myself to see what others might describe as sound, hear the most tantalizing odiferous sensations, taste and touch my way to new and exhilarating experiences. I am not alone, either.

I am reminded of the insightful Walt Whitman poem, "There Was a Child Went Forth." It opens with these perceptive lines:

There was a child went forth every day;
   And the first object he look'd upon, that object he became;
   And that object became part of him for the day, or a certain
part of the day, or for many years, or stretching cycles of years.

As grown-ups, we have the advantage of internalizing and reinventing our experiences. It can alter our reality and free us to move beyond our own personal needs and limitations. I believe the destination is in the self-fulfilling realm of sensory awareness. It is there the inspirations we long for await interpretation and activation. Still, missing from the mix is the essence of magical thinking. It requires leading with the heart. I call it love.[5]

The twentieth-century humanist Franklin P. Jones said it even more philosophically:

Love doesn't make the world go 'round.
Love is what makes the ride worthwhile.

1. I continue to be involved with Women's Project Theatre as chair emeritus of the board and in 2015 was elected to its newly formed Founder's Circle. I support Carnegie Hall, as well as a myriad of programs at Lincoln Center (ballet, opera, theater, and music). I am a devotee of the Broadway stage. Priority membership includes the Whitney Museum, the Metropolitan Museum of Art, the Museum of Modern Art, the Morgan Library, and the National Arts Club.

   I also participate in several organizations, including the International Fashion Group, Cosmetic Executive Women and Women's Forum, the Noel Coward Society, Roundabout Theatre Company, Manhattan Theatre Club, and Food for Thought.

   In the last few years, I've visited Paris, South Africa, Vietnam, Cambodia, and Thailand, and sailed to the Netherlands, the South of France, and Saint Petersburg, Russia. One of my most recent visits was to Cuba, which I first experienced in the late fifties.

   I consult on myriad projects and have been invited to speak about my career and the fragrance industry to various organizations, including the International Perfume Bottle Collectors Club, of which I am also an honorary member.

   One of the most interesting new involvements is my presence on the Influence Advisory Board of a highly lauded avant-garde agency, Sparks & Honey, a division of Omnicom. Its groundbreaking work in cultural trend identification and analysis around the world (using proprietary cultural mapping methodologies) has placed it in the forefront of preparing a broad cross section of industries to meet the dynamic social changes taking place globally.

2. **The Fragrance/Fashion Promenade** (see chapter II)

   Definitely rethinkable. The medium, however, might well be cable. I can imagine a show starring fashions that express the latest fragrances or products from a wide variety of other categories.

   Annette Green Perfume Museum (see chapter IV)

   And what a great moment this could be to create a virtual perfume museum inspired by the one and only in existence at the Fashion Institute of Design & Merchandising in LA. What a meaningful way to reach an international audience!

   FiFi Awards (see chapter III)

   The appeal of recognizing excellence in all the creative arts from music to theater and motion pictures to fragrances has no expiration date.

   Fashion Institute of Technology (see chapter V)

   The benefits of an educated workforce have been proven beyond the shadow of a doubt by FIT here in New York with its bachelor's and master's programs in beauty and fragrance marketing. They could certainly be replicated in other universities here and abroad.

   Fragrance Fun Day (see chapter IX)

   The tremendous sensory potential of FFD could be reinterpreted to appeal to the public in cities throughout the world to help counter the challenges of online shopping.

   Certification Program (see chapter XI)

Now, here's a program that could work for the public and for the industry. It could not only be dedicated to educating sales specialists but also students and consumers. Training degrees might be established with major industries in each city to recognize up-and-coming talent that has fulfilled a prescribed mandate.

Sense of Smell Institute (see chapter XII)

There could be no better time to support and report on the ongoing scientific studies of the brain and the role of the senses in maintaining physical, as well as psychological, well-being at every age.

National Fragrance Week (see chapter XV)

As consumers spend less and less time in stores and more time on the internet, Fragrance Week could be a perfect vehicle to entertain the public with surprising sensory experiences in cities across the country.

Summit 2000 (see chapter XVI)

The emergence of the first global society could be reinterpreted decade by decade, in cooperation with social media and think tanks specializing in future trends. A possible partner could be the *Economist*, Sparks & Honey, and/or futurist Edith Weiner.

3. Jean-Baptiste Alphonse Karr (1808–1890) made his reputation as a French critic, journalist, editor of *Le Figaro*, and prolific novelist. He also founded and edited a satirical monthly journal, *Les Guepes* (the *Wasps*), in which he first coined his famous proverb "Plus ça change, plus c'est la même chose." In 1855, M. Alphonse Karr moved to Nice and devoted himself to "floralculture" and is credited with establishing the trade in cut flowers on the French Riviera.

4. For me, the light went on when I was a young journalist in the late fifties. I was assigned to interview a child psychologist. She shared many fascinating revelations, but the one I have never forgotten was her unequivocal declaration, "To be successful in life, one must be able to hear the grass growing." I wasn't sure what she meant, but it inspired me to think and rethink and finally understand and apply her meaning.

   In review of the American Ballet Theatre's production of *Cinderella* in spring 2015, *New York Times* critic Alastair Macaulay noted in his concluding critique, "The more closely you listen to the production, the more you see." *Oh,* I thought, *he really gets it! How wonderful!*

5. In this spirit, I committed myself to wearing a small gold "love" pin every day for the past forty-plus years. Originally a token of affection, it unfailing evokes a warmhearted response not only from friends and colleagues but from strangers, as well. When asked about it, I simply respond, "That's my message."

Special Appreciation

Thank you to Linda Levy, President of the Fragrance Foundation for permission to include excerpts from the quarterly Fragrance Forum, which I wrote and edited from 1984 through its final issue in 2002.

I also want to remember early picture-takers who memorialized my journey—Eli Aaron, Al Levine, Walter Herstadt, Gould Studios, Wagner International and the endlessly courteous, intuitive and talented photographer who covered the momentous moments in the last half of my career, Eric T. Michaelson.

Thanks for the Memories

The Remarkable Fragrance Foundation Team

Mary Ellen Lapsansky, Vice President

My career at the Fragrance Foundation started in 1989, working directly for Annette Green, then executive director of the foundation. The foundation opened the door to many rewarding and unique experiences within the fragrance industry. It afforded me a fresh perspective on the creative process and a true appreciation of fragrance in all its forms. I was given entrée to a world not accessible to many industry people. And this was, of course, due to Annette's iconic stature.

When I had come on board, the foundation was coming to grips with how to meet the needs of its members as we were fast approaching the twenty-first century. Focus groups had been established to address the future direction of the foundation in relation to its program, initiatives, and outreach. As a result of these focus groups, two major initiatives/programs were established: the European Fragrance Foundation licensees and the certification program for fragrance sales specialists. I was directly involved in both from their inceptions, which proved to be challenging, as well as gratifying.

I saw the foundation expand and morph over the years to a truly global organization with licensees in the EU, Australia, and Japan. The certification program also was able to expand its reach through the development of an online program. And Fragrance Week went national—to fourteen cities across the United States.

Of course, the highlight of each year was the magical FiFi Awards which, at its height, attracted an audience of sixteen hundred international guests. It was always exhilarating to help organize the awards ceremony, especially the year it was held at Radio City Music Hall with the Rockettes.

There was never a dull moment in the planning of this key industry event each year.

Working with Annette, whose passion was contagious and ideas ever-flowing, was an experience like no other. We worked as a team on so many new initiatives and programs—for our members, the industry at large, and most important, the consumer.

Those were the days!

Theresa Molnar, Director

In 1999, after a job search, I joined the Fragrance Foundation. I was frankly trying to steer away from the fragrance and cosmetics industry. Having spent the previous fifteen years at Fabergé in various positions in sales and marketing, I was ready to explore new horizons when the company was sold to Chesebrough Ponds. Nevertheless, at the suggestion of Amelia Bassin, a former Fabergé marketing guru, I sent my résumé off to Annette Green and pretty much forgot about it until she contacted me six months later, informing me that there was an opening at the Fragrance Foundation if I was still interested. As my unemployment was running out, I figured I had nothing to lose by at least seeing what the job was about. In one of the shortest job interviews I've ever had, Annette briefly described the position of executive administrator of what was then called the Fragrance Foundation Research Fund.

Annette pretty much told me the job was mine if I wanted it. I was somewhat reluctant, as it involved coordinating scientific research grants, working with sensory psychologists and other scientists, organizing scientific symposia, and more. I had no scientific background or experience with any of this, but with Annette's encouragement, I decided to take up the challenge. Yes, it was still in the fragrance industry, but this was totally new and admittedly intriguing territory that was far removed from my previous experience in the business.

I spent the first few months asking myself what the heck I'd gotten myself into as I learned the ropes. But Annette's passion for fragrance and enthusiasm about building a unique charitable organization devoted to exploring the science of olfaction and the benefits of fragrance on human behavior turned out to be contagious, and I was soon drawn in. At the same time, as I read grant applications and research reports and I interacted with the researchers themselves, I was pulled into the fascinating world of sensory psychology and neuroscience. The science geek in me was born.

There was never a dull moment over the next twelve years working with Annette, the researchers, and the advisory board with what ultimately became the Sense of Smell Institute and the Fragrance Foundation team. Every day presented fresh opportunities to learn, and new horizons were opened at every turn. Ideas for new projects and programs for both organizations were constantly floated and discussed, which resulted in a multifaceted, multitasking workplace. What I found most rewarding were the education programs we developed for the adult public, as well as for schoolchildren, where it became obvious there was natural interest in the subject of olfaction and how our emotions and sense of smell are so intertwined. Our annual Sense of Smell Day events at science and children's museums across the country and our annual career guidance fair for high school students were stellar among these programs.

If I had to summarize my experience in the decade-plus that I worked with Annette and the Sense of Smell Institute, I'd say it was an ongoing learning experience, enlightening, thought-provoking, stimulating, challenging, and ultimately rewarding in every sense.

Ina Gray, Office Manager

In August 1970, I started at Ms. Green's public relations agency, Annette Green Associates, as a clerk typist. I remember the day of the job interview at 101 Park Avenue. It was raining really hard, and I was dripping wet but still showed up for the interview. To make matters worse, I got lost because I did not know my way around the city. Ms. Berk interviewed me, but when it came time to do the typing test, she looked at me and said, "Don't worry about the typing." (This is just to show the type of caring person she was.)

At that time, the Fragrance Foundation was a client. Some years later when the agency closed and transitioned full-time to the Fragrance Foundation, I became an employee and worked there for thirty-three years.

The Fragrance Foundation was the pioneer organization for the fragrances introduced in America and later developed into a worldwide organization under the leadership of Ms. Green, who by that time had been appointed the president. I later became the office manager and, in this position, was responsible for the processing of new member applications and membership renewals, overseeing the affairs of the office, and interfacing with staff on major projects, including special events, meetings, and seminars. I was also actively involved in National Fragrance Week activities and the awards ball ceremony. I enjoyed the work I did at the foundation.

One of my most memorable days at the foundation was one day when we were preparing for the awards ball, and the phone rang. I answered it, and the caller asked to speak to Annette Green. I asked who was calling, and he said, "Bill Clinton." I said, "What company are you with?" He said it was *President* Clinton. I was so surprised that I forgot to say, "Please hold," and I dropped the phone, ran to AG's office, and screamed, "President Clinton is on the phone!"

I learned so much about fragrances through the teachings of Ms. Green and her dedicated partner, Lois Berk. Ms. Berk was very easygoing and had a great sense of humor. I could go to her with any problem, and she would find a solution. The entire staff missed her tremendously when she passed.

Because of the close relationship with Annette Green, over the years we became like family. And although the rest of the staff called her Miss Green, we developed the loving nickname AG. To this day, all members of my family, including the grandchildren, call her AG with pride.

She taught me collegial interactions with the membership, the press, and the consumer. I will always treasure the great memories.

Lilia B. Nicoletti, Administrator

When I started to collect miniature perfume bottles many years ago, I became part of the world of fragrance. Then, one day in 2000, I walked into the Fragrance Foundation for a job interview, and much to my surprise, the reception area had the most beautiful display of "factices." And just as I discovered that my tiny bottles had huge counterparts, I met Annette Green, president of the Fragrance Foundation—a petite person with a huge passion for all that defines the word *fragrance*.

We were all dedicated to make the mission of the Fragrance Foundation a reality at every opportunity with every event, big or small. I had the pleasure of working with Annette side by side, especially on those long days just prior to the FiFis, when every single detail had her touch. I went along, always trying to learn how to develop my own passion! After all these years ... well, I am still walking behind Annette as she marches on the yellow brick road!

I am very grateful for all the opportunities she always afforded me.

Wind Under My Wings

Set your life on fire.
Seek those who fan your flames.

—Rumi

Bouquets to all the mentors, supporters, and heavenly angels you have just met on the pages of my book. Loving appreciation, too, to family, friends, and colleagues who encouraged me to fly higher than I could ever have imagined, before, during, and after my sojourn in the fragrance world. Burt Bachrach Sr., Donald Bauchner, Marian Bendeth, Peter Block, Mike Blumenfeld, Pete Born, Tova Bourgnine, Margot Brandau, Rose Marie Bravo, Alan Burke, Jessica Canne, Gerry Cohen, Dale Crichton, Jim Dellas, Carmen Dell'Orefice, Adelaide Farah, Gary Farn, Marvin Feldman, Ruth Findley, Patrick Firmenich, Dorothy Foster, Greg Furman, Helen Galland, Joe Garces, Grace Gaynor, Lillian Gilden, Dorothy Globus, Rena and Richard Golub, William, Harry, and Samuel Green, Susan Hayes, Richard and Elsie Hirsch, Gertrude Ukrainsky, Herta deKreith, Catherine Hunter, Freda Kaufman, E. Edward Kavanugh, Pauline Kenarik, Jack Kirkman, Barbara Kotlicoff, Elizabeth Kunke, Leonard and Evelyn Lauder, Richard Lockman, Shirley Lord, Michel Mane, Mary Manning, Eileen McCarthy, Eleanor McVickar, Pablo Medina, Sunny Miller, Jean-Claude Moreau, Westly Morris, Allan Mottus, Marilyn Munder, Luciano and Rosetta Parasini, Bernice Peck, Laurice Rahme, Milton Raynor, Valli Schartzchild, Eleanor and Al Seares, Bobby Short, Leonard Sloane, Elizabeth Sobieski Carmen Solis, Errol Stafford, Dan Stebbins, Leonard Stoller, Billie Sutter, Bruce Teitelbaum, Craig Thompson, Demi Thoman, Lawrence Wechsler, June Weir, Jim Wesley, and most especially Lois Berk,[1] my brilliant, enduring, endearing alter ego, who never left a stone unturned in the pursuit of excellence. She was the perfect combination of dedication, wit, and wisdom. I couldn't have done it without her. And kudos to Sherry

Manquis for her nose-to-the-grindstone assistance in helping me translate my thoughts to the printed page; my first editor, Victoria Wright, who treated every word and phrase with loving and elucidating care and a very special shout out to my computer guru, Joseph Small, who not only solved every glitch along the way; but helped me format *Spritzing to Success* with grace and style. Last but not least, kudos to the Sparks and Honey team – Terry Young and Annalie Killian, as well as Bryan Janeczko and lola Killian for their extraordinary support and expertise.

---

1. Tribute by Dr. Fernando Aleu, 1993 (Winter issue of the *Fragrance Forum*):
   "Lois Berk, who served with such devotion as executive administrator and factotum extraordinaire of the Fragrance Foundation for thirty-two years, has left us. It is our great loss. Most members of the foundation knew her; few knew her well. What a pity!
   "She was a woman of inner grace, bright, concerned and caring. She was a perpetual understatement while quietly over-performing in every endeavor. She had for her inner circle a great sense of humor. She was discreet, quiet, and omnipresent. An effective problem solver with the additional gift of making people feel important even if they were not. She had many more qualities, but one that I admired greatly was her command of English. She respected and loved our language, something that is becoming a rare quality. Above all: she was fair. Lois never left a phone call unanswered or greeted a visitor without a smile.
   "She did smoke, and she did smoke a lot, but when everything is taken in perspective what we would not give today for whiff of her secondhand smoke.
   "We will miss her. We will miss her a lot."